FIRST COMES
LOVE

THEN COMES
MONEY

FIRST COMES
LOVE

THEN COMES
MONEY

*Basic Steps to Avoid the #1
Conflict in Marriage*

ROGER GIBSON

New Leaf Press

First printing, October 1998

ISBN: 0-89221-418-X
Library of Congress Catalog No. 98-66298

Scripture quotations, unless otherwise indicated, are from *The Living Bible*.

Cover by Left Coast Design, Portland, OR.

Printed in the United States of America.

TO MY WIFE: KARI LYNN

Thank you for your love the past 15 years, your endless encouragement, and most of all for showing me the way to the Cross.

TO MY SON: MICHAEL THOMAS

Thank you for the endless smiles, laughter, and fun you bring to my life. God has truly blessed me with a son that I always dreamed of having.

TO MY DAUGHTER: HANNAH ELISE

Thank you for coming into my life. Your early start in life, only weighing two pounds, has taught me the real meaning of FAITH. Joy in my life would never have been complete without you.

TO MY PARENTS: MOM AND DAD

From tiny-tot soccer games to the presentation of this book, you two have always been right behind me cheering me on. Thank you for giving me a life of love.

TO MY WIFE'S PARENTS: MOM AND DAD II

The greatest givers I know. Proud to be your son-in-law, and thank you for loving me as a son.

ACKNOWLEDGMENTS

WOW! Thinking back to all the people in my life that have had an impact on me, I can't help but say, "WOW!" God has blessed me in many ways, starting with the second greatest gift I could have ever received (next to knowing Jesus Christ), my wife, Kari. The book could have never been completed without her encouragement and permission to write about our screw-ups.

Thanks to a special group of people who have left their mark of wisdom, love, and encouragement: Randy and Tracy Williams; Guy and Debbie Romero; my college basketball coach, Michael Maker; my college pastor, Ike Riddle; my high school basketball coach, Bob Fredricks; Gary and Christy Lee; Jamie Coston; Keith Blue; Brett Loehmann; Don Munton; John Trent; Jim Brawner; and Terry Brown. A special thanks to my brother, Riff, a little brother's dream.

I need to give thanks to all the money and marriage experts who not only have had an impact on my life, but also on thousands of others. I hope this book is able to touch lives in the same way you have.

To my friends who have read and given great insights into the book: John and Marianne Webster, Billy and Kathy Ong, Terry and Janna Brown, Clancy Parks, Wendy Davidson, Sheila Smethers, Kent and Lori Vanderpool, Pamela Spears, Doug and Dee Goodwin, Greg and Julie Baker, Greg Smalley, and Mark and Angie Pyatt.

The greatest thing to come out of writing this book are my new friends at New Leaf Press, who not only know how to work, but know how to have fun. Thank you, Tim Dudley, for your support, encouragement, and friendship. Jim Fletcher and Val Cindric, my editors, who were great at getting the book just the way I envisioned it. Dianna, Timothy, Janell, and Judy, thanks for all the hard work you put into the book.

CONTENTS

FOREWORD

UNRESOLVED arguments kill more marriages than any other problem. What do couples argue about most? Money.

Every day couples have to make numerous financial decisions: Should I go to work or take a sick day? Which bills can I pay? Are we saving enough for the future?

Like mixing drinking and driving together, money and marriage can be a deadly combination.

My wife, Norma, and I had our own conflicts regarding money in the beginning years of our marriage. As newlyweds, we fell right in with the millions of other starry-eyed couples. We mixed marriage with money, and it almost wrecked us.

I was not very responsible financially. Growing up, I had never learned how, or even realized, that proper money management mattered. I didn't know anything about keeping a checkbook register or spending wisely.

Norma, on the other hand, was a detail-oriented person who worked at a bank. It was obvious that she should keep the family books and pay the bills, which she was happy to do.

The problems arose right at the start and lasted five years. Each of us had a checkbook and wrote checks on one joint account. You can imagine the confusion this caused.

I had my own system: I wrote checks as long as I had them in my book or until the checks ran out. I hoped or assumed there was enough in the bank to cover them.

Too often Norma would confront me. "Are you aware that we're overdrawn again?"

"We can't be," I'd answer with a grin. "I still have checks in my book. It's impossible."

Sometimes she would be in tears. "I can't keep track of this," she'd say. "It's driving me crazy."

We also had a secondary conflict. We disagreed about *when* to pay the bills. Norma preferred to pay them as soon as they came. I wanted to hold on to our money as long as possible, paying our bills at the end of the month, just before payday. I liked the idea of having money because you never know when an emergency might come up. With my check-writing habits, however, there wasn't always enough left at the end of the month to pay all the bills — let alone extra for emergencies.

"We have two late notices on this one bill," Norma would say, exasperated.

"Don't worry," I told her. "You don't have to do anything until you get the fourth or fifth notice. Just keep shuffling late notices to the bottom of the pile until they appear at the top again and can't be ignored any longer."

By-the-book Norma found this kind of aberrant financial philosophy appalling to say the least.

Finally, the day came when Norma reached the end of her rope. She tearfully approached me once more and laid all the bills, her checkbook, and the budget in my lap.

"I've had it," she declared. "I can't take it anymore. From now on this is your problem. It's up to you whether we sink or swim."

Years later, she admitted her despair that day. "I figured I was giving away our home, our car, and the rest of our financial life," she told me. "I knew there was no way you would be able to handle our finances properly."

Fortunately, with the pressure on, I decided to learn how to be responsible. I got some help, grew to respect a budget, and worked my way out of the mess I had created. For the next 15 years, I kept the books and paid the bills.

As I started to do all this, I learned a crucial but simple principle: You've got to have more money in the bank than you spend every month. Simple as that solution sounds, it was a profound revelation to me.

Repairing the damage done to our relationship, however, posed a more difficult challenge. As you can imagine, Norma and I needed a lot of help to resolve this major conflict in our marriage.

That same type of help is available for you today through Roger Gibson's new book, *First Comes Love, Then Comes Money.*

Roger shares humorous — yet painful — stories from his own

marriage and outlines easy steps to prevent conflict before it happens. He also explains a communication method that will immediately reduce money arguments between you and your mate. As you learn how to identify the money strengths and weaknesses which you and your mate possess, your marriage will experience a new burst of freedom.

You will also discover a realistic spending plan that will not only help you gain control of your spending but help you reach your dreams. And, after all, isn't that what marriage is all about?

— Gary Smalley

CHAPTER ONE
LOVE & MONEY

KARI and I had been married only two weeks when we experienced our first financial conflict. In fact, we could still hear the church bells chiming when the shots rang out!

After a beautiful, fairy-tale wedding, we had excitedly — and cautiously — anticipated our honeymoon. Our friends had told us their honeymoon "horror stories," so we were prepared for the worst.

"If we can survive our week-long trip to the beach," I told Kari, "we can survive anything together."

To our surprise, we didn't have one glitch in our plans. Every flight arrived on time, our luggage repeatedly appeared first on the conveyor belt, and the weather stayed perfect all week. We did get sunburned on the last day, but that didn't dampen our spirits. When we stepped off the plane, we were still flying high from our nearly perfect honeymoon.

After returning to earth, Kari and I moved into our new house to begin the journey of marriage. As we settled into our life together, it never occurred to us that the joy and stability of our relationship would soon be sorely tested.

We had married just three months after my college graduation. The month before our wedding I got a job as a financial advisor for a national company. With my college education I was ready to take on the world and help people gain financial freedom.

Kari had been teaching at an elementary school for two years prior to our marriage and was making a good salary. Our plan was to use her income to pay for the living expenses until I received my first commission. I couldn't wait to start raking in the big bucks at my new corporate job. At the end of the first month, however, I had not received a paycheck. Although disappointed, I was optimistic about several important appointments scheduled for the next couple of days. I felt confident I would meet our company's standard criteria with these new "possible" clients.

JUST WHAT I ALWAYS WANTED!

One hot, humid afternoon I had an appointment on the west side of Phoenix. If you have ever been in Arizona during the summer, you know that an air-conditioned car is a vital necessity to get from point A to B without major dehydration. Unfortunately, I owned an older model with a temperamental air conditioner. The cool air would go on and off regularly, so I never knew what to expect.

On this particular day the air conditioner was in an "off" mood. In fact, I had not experienced a cool day all week. To avoid being drenched with perspiration, I took off my shirt and tie for the 15-minute drive to my appointment.

After the meeting, I stepped outside and noticed an auto mall next to the office building. Since I had a couple of hours before my next appointment, I decided to kill some time by looking at all the new, shiny vehicles.

As I casually strolled through the lot, something awesome caught my eye. I spotted my "dream" truck. Its dark green paint sparkled in the intense sunlight beckoning me in that direction.

"Man, this is just what I've always wanted!" I said out loud. "A full-size, extended cab with all the extras."

I envisioned myself roaring up rocky mountains and splashing through muddy puddles in my new four-wheel drive — just like in the TV commercials.

As I climbed into the driver's side, a salesman appeared from out of nowhere. Smiling, he studied my startled face. He had seen dozens of glassy-eyed customers sitting in this very spot and kindly offered, "How'd you like to take this baby for a spin around the block?"

The spider had spun his web.

As soon as I turned on the ignition, I flipped the air conditioner to full blast and felt the cold air immediately hit me in the face.

The salesman jumped in the passenger side, and I was off. I had always wanted to know how it felt to drive a big truck. It drove powerfully, yet smoothly around the quiet neighborhood.

This is exactly how I dreamed it would be, I told myself.

Although the salesman was turning blue from the arctic air blasting out of the vents, I felt exhilarated.

After returning to the lot, I planned to head off to my next appointment. The salesman, however, had a different plan.

Once he had thawed out, he managed to finish off any restraint I might have had: "How would you like to own this truck?"

The only response I could muster was, "Sure, I'd love to, but I don't think I can afford it."

He responded confidently, "I think you'll be surprised. I'll bet I can find you a good deal on this truck."

I love a good deal, so I decided to follow him to the sales office to hear a few details for "future" reference. Since I had an appointment soon, I knew I could escape.

I gave him about two minutes to share his enthusiastic sales pitch, then I jumped up, thanked him for his time, and mentioned I had an appointment.

"Can I use your phone to let my contact know I'm on my way?" I asked.

As I spoke to my prospective client's secretary, she told me the appointment had been canceled. I rescheduled the meeting for the following day.

Realizing I was now without an excuse to flee the salesman's office, I sat down and listened to the remainder of his talk.

"So, Roger," he asked pointedly, "are you interested in buying the truck?"

"It sounds great," I stammered, "but I just graduated from college and got married two weeks ago. In fact, I haven't even received a paycheck from my new job."

By throwing out these few major details, I was quite certain he wouldn't want to sell me a car. His response, however, was just the opposite.

"No problem," he said simply.

We had now entered the negotiation phase. Since I love to haggle, this aspect of the procedure became a real challenge.

The salesman gave me an initial price for the truck. It was too high, so I gave him my price. I knew my numbers were too low and still thought I could walk away from this harmless situation without any trouble.

For an entire hour we went back and forth. Finally, we ended up with an amount that was far lower than my initial offer.

I couldn't believe my ears. Was it really possible for me to buy a truck without even having a salary? It was unbelievable. What a country!

I instantly realized this was too great a deal to pass up, and the rationalization process began.

I'm so tired and hot driving that old car. I need a new vehicle, I told myself. I decided to "go for it!"

A DEAL OF A LIFETIME?

One hour later I drove out of the lot with my "dream" truck. I couldn't wait to get home and surprise my newlywed wife.

My anticipation soared higher and higher the closer I got to home. Turning the last corner to our block, I began honking wildly.

As I pulled into our driveway, not only did Kari come running out, the entire neighborhood rushed to see what the commotion was all about.

Kari had a look of horror on her face as she stammered, "Where did you get this truck?"

"I just bought it!" I said proudly.

"You did what?" Kari sputtered.

"I bought it! I got the deal of a lifetime." I shouted, still smiling.

"You have got to be kidding . . ." Kari whispered.

"No! I really bought the truck. Don't you just love it?" I asked, oblivious to her confusion.

For the first time in her life, Kari was speechless. The look on her face, however, spoke volumes. I am sure she must have been

GOD CANNOT GIVE US HAPPINESS AND PEACE
APART FROM HIMSELF, BECAUSE IT IS NOT THERE.
THERE IS NO SUCH THING.

C.S. LEWIS (1898-1963)

thinking, *How can anyone go out and buy a brand new truck without first talking with his wife?*

Silently she walked back into the house.

After the tension lessened and Kari regained her voice, she asked me, "How are we going to pay for that truck?"

"I used the gift money from your dad as a down payment and then financed the rest," I explained.

Without fully realizing it at the time, I had managed, in less than two hours, to possibly cause serious damage to my new marriage.

I had put Kari and myself immediately into major debt. Cruising off the lot that day, I had driven our marriage right into the repair shop.

It didn't take long for the excitement of getting a new truck and the thrill of seeing it in our driveway to turn sour. The moment of truth had arrived.

All evening Kari had tried to put on a brave face. Finally, as we prepared for bed she asked, "Isn't that an expensive truck?" Then, trying to steady her shaky voice, she continued, "Are you sure we can afford it? You haven't even received a paycheck from your new job."

As I pondered those three important facts — the same ones I had shared with the salesman only hours before — I rapidly realized that I had made a terrible mistake. I spent a sleepless night tossing and turning and wondering how in the world I ever got myself into this mess.

Here we were, only two weeks into married life, and I had created a financial situation that put terrible stress on our relationship. Kari felt betrayed, and I felt like a jerk. In fact, this experience was one of the most painful and embarrassing moments of my life.

After all, I had majored in finance and was working to become a financial advisor. How could I have gotten myself into this?

By buying a new truck I imposed added pressure on Kari and myself by putting us into debt for five years to pay for a vehicle that I really did not need. To make matters worse, I had failed to consult with Kari before purchasing the vehicle.

SHOWDOWN IN THE SHOWROOM

Three sleepless nights into our dilemma, Kari and I decided it would be best if I took the truck to the dealer and got our money back. As I gathered all the nerve I hoped I had, I drove the truck up to the dealer's parking lot and headed into the showroom to get back my down payment — just as if nothing had ever happened!

As I explained my story to the first available salesman, I could tell by the look on his face that he couldn't wait to tell the other guys about my predicament.

After I finished my painful tale, he said, "I'll have to get the manager on duty."

Once again I explained my desire to exchange the truck for the down payment. "After all, the truck is only three days old," I added.

As the manager pondered my proposal, he came back with, "I can't exchange the truck for your down payment because the bank has already processed the loan. But I can take a trade-in for the truck and give you another car that is worth your down payment."

I could only imagine what awaited me on "The Lot of Unwanted Cars." How was I going to explain this to Kari? When I left home that morning, I had told her not to worry. I knew what I was doing.

As I considered all the options, I decided to accept his offer and handed over the keys to my dream truck. They led me out (sounds like an execution, huh?) to the used cars and showed me all the possibilities available — one.

The manager pointed to a light blue, four-door sedan with a big fuzzy steering wheel.

My old car was better than this, I thought.

As I got in the car and started it up, tears rolled down my cheeks. *How could this have happened*, I kept asking myself. *I'm sure Kari is going to be disappointed in me.*

This time when I approached the house I tried to figure out how I could camouflage my "classic" four-door sedan. In fact, I was thinking of ways to sell the house, so I wouldn't have to face our neighbors. I pulled the car into the driveway and sprinted into the house. Without saying a word to Kari, I threw the keys down and proceeded toward the couch to try and erase the humiliating event from my memory.

In her enthusiasm, Kari wanted to know what happened. "It can't be that bad. Tell me about it."

"We cleared ourselves, and I got a car for the amount of the down payment," I said halfheartedly.

Pleased, she ran outside to look at the car. A couple of minutes passed. Her laughter ricocheted off the walls as she staggered back inside. Once I saw her laughing, I started to laugh, and we doubled over until our faces were numb.

"What *is* that?" Kari finally managed.

Relieved by my wife's hilarious reaction, I decided to accept our fate and get on with my life.

The next day, Kari was on the phone with her dad who was in another state. When she shared what had happened, he reacted like a protective bear with cubs. "I can't believe what that dealer did!" he exclaimed and placed his own phone call without my knowledge.

When the general manager came on the line, my father-in-law bellowed, "I can't believe you would take advantage of a young man the way you did! I am going to go on radio and TV telling people what type of business you run."

The general manager reacted defensively: "Hold on! What did we do?"

After Gary shared the entire incident with him, the general manager said, "Send your son-in-law over, and I'll take care of everything."

Excitedly, Gary called me and shared that the general manager wanted to straighten out the horrible mistake.

"When will this nightmare end?" I mumbled as I hung up the phone. I thought I was finished making a fool of myself. Now I had to go back and be put on display again. Step right up, and see the Idiot Boy!

Again, I summoned my nerve — this time to meet with the general manager. I told him the whole story — start to finish. As I recognized a sign of sympathy rising in his face, I tried to milk it for everything I could.

"I can't give you a new truck," he told me, "but I can find a used truck for roughly the same amount."

As I was walking out the door, the general manager made a suggestion: "Tell your father-in-law he may want to take anger management classes, or someday he's going to die of a heart attack."

I had to chuckle. Normally, my father-in-law is the most fun-loving guy I know.

A week passed, and I had yet to get a call from the general manager about a used truck. When I phoned, he told me they still had not located one. Not wanting to drive the four-door sedan with the fuzzy steering wheel any longer than necessary, I persisted and called every day for two weeks. Finally, the general manager told me to meet him that afternoon.

At the appointed time, he pumped my hand and said, "I am going to give you a brand new truck. Not a four-wheel drive, but a two-wheel pick-up. Will that make it even?"

I assured him it would!

I picked out a candy-apple red truck. Only one problem: the truck had no air-conditioning (the whole reason for a new car).

Turning to the exasperated general manager, I said, "I would like to get air-conditioning installed."

"You can have it," he sighed.

Feeling like Aladdin gliding away on his carpet, I roared out of the lot with the arctic blast in my face.

THE MONEY MARATHON

A recent Gallop poll found that 56 percent of all divorces are related to financial tension in the home.

If you are newly married, you should face the fact that — no matter how hard you try to avoid it — money will always be a factor in your life and in your marriage.

Marriage and finances are much like a marathon: It (seemingly) never ends. Permit me to dwell on this analogy for a moment.

After training for six months and running six days a week, I chose Houston for my first marathon event.

I anticipated a sunny day, but the weather was terrible with pouring rain and sleet. The roads were covered with ice.

As the gun sounded and the runners started, I took my place and began to move my feet. The first mile all the runners crowded together, surrounding me as they jockeyed for position.

After mile three, everyone began to spread out, and each runner had his space. The first six miles were great.

I can finish this with no problem, I told myself, feeling as if I could run forever.

When I hit mile 20, however, I was tired, cold, and sore. The miles seemed to have lengthened, and the drive to finish had diminished.

Then, as I came closer to the finish line, the cheers from the crowd became louder and louder. My legs somehow gained more strength in an effort to push my body to the end of the 26.2-mile run.

As I turned the final corner, I could see the words "FINISH" on the top of a big banner marking the end of the race. With my eyes focused on the magical line, I began to run faster and faster (which is actually an illusion). As I crossed the finish line, the thrill of finishing was all the reward I needed.

The money marathon in marriage often takes on the character of a race. At times, the pressure can become too intense, and many couples want to throw in the towel and quit before the finish line comes into view. Like any marathon, you have to pace yourself and keep focused on your final goal.

It would be foolish for a marathon runner to expend all his energy by sprinting as fast as possible in the first few miles. He would never make it to the end.

Many young married couples, however, break all the rules "to get it all" in the beginning. They overload themselves with debt by buying everything new during their first few years of marriage. This no-holds-barred approach quickly wears thin and can cause the "tie that binds" to snap and knock you off balance.

The stress of poor money management puts added pressure on what should be one of the happiest and most enjoyable times of your lives. Instead, you find yourselves arguing about spending habits, credit card debt, and unpaid bills. Add to that worry about the future, and you have the recipe for marital distress.

In this book, I want to give you some tools to help lessen the

HAPPINESS IS AS A BUTTERFLY, WHICH, WHEN PURSUED IS ALWAYS JUST BEYOND OUR GRASP, BUT WHICH, IF YOU WILL SIT DOWN QUIETLY, MAY ALIGHT UPON YOU.

NATHANIEL HAWTHORNE
(1804–1864)

divorce risk created by financial tension. These simple steps can resolve the most prevalent source of contention among married couples — money — and keep your marriage headed toward the goals that matter most in life.

DETERMINING YOUR GOALS

In the beginning of my marriage, I put us in debt and out of harmony by making a non-mutual financial decision. Buying a truck doesn't happen every day in most marriages, but situations involving money occur day in and day out.

A purchase at a shopping mall may spark an argument that can last for days. Credit card bills can create ongoing conflicts. The constant need to supply a lifestyle currently out of your reach can cause division, pulling one or both partners away from the home in an effort to make more money. All of these potentially dangerous situations can quickly undermine a marriage.

Since you are reading this book, I assume you want answers to existing or potential financial conflicts in your marriage. If so, I suggest you begin by determining where your problems lie and what you want to do about them.

Which of these goals apply to you and your marriage?

1. I want to pay off my credit cards and get out of debt.

2. I want to get a better understanding of my expenses so I'm not always behind in paying my bills.

3. I want to learn to resolve conflicts without hurting my mate's feelings.

4. I want to learn how to be more dependent upon God than money.

5. I want to change my spending habits.

6. I want to learn how I can become more pro-active in my finances.

7. I want to understand why my mate handles money the way he or she does.

If these examples don't fit your personal goals, I urge you to make your own list. The best way to fix something is to determine what needs fixing.

What is the first step to gaining financial freedom? More income? Better investments? An organized system? All of these help, but the first step begins with *you*. You first need to learn more about yourself — your financial temperament, your strengths and weaknesses, your past — the elements that have created your money "shape."

Effective change only begins from the inside out. Once you know what areas need to be changed, you can begin resolving these money management issues and the conflicts they now cause in your marriage.

Later chapters provide valuable tools to help you relieve the money pressures in your life. Before these tools can work for you, however, you need to learn what motivates you to make certain financial decisions,

In the next chapter you will begin the journey of making changes inside out, starting with the exciting adventure of understanding your money personality.

Later, I will share the secrets for a fulfilling life that neither money, jewelry, clothes, nor jobs can ever come close to attaining. As you begin the journey to financial harmony in your marriage, I urge you to seek God's direction throughout the book.

CHAPTER TWO
YOUR MONEY PERSONALITY

This evening, I looked eastward over the Pacific. . . . I shall be glad when we have the hazards of its navigation behind us. — Amelia Earhart.

WHEN I was growing up, my mother was a flight attendant. As a result, I never experienced family vacations from the back seat of a station wagon. Instead, I usually sat in the back of an airplane.

Even my first trip to college took place on a 737. With all my possessions packed in one suitcase, I bravely said goodbye to my family for the trip to California.

Like any freshman I was nervous about leaving home and going to another state. In an effort to relax, I anxiously took deep breaths and watched out the window as the familiarity of Arizona faded beneath me.

Before long, the flight attendant began asking passengers what they wanted to drink. As she parked her beverage cart next to my seat, she opened her mouth to ask me the same question.

Suddenly, we hit an air pocket! The plane dropped for what seemed like an eternity. While my heart and stomach stayed up in the atmosphere, my body shot down with the plane!

At the same time, drinks on the cart flew into the air and — instead of returning to their rightful place — landed all over me. I was soaked with Coke and Diet Coke — but at least I was alive! What I had imagined to be "the end" was merely a "speed bump" in the sky.

That was only one of many bumpy rides I have experienced over the years, but it's the one I have never forgotten. In fact, whenever life throws me a curve and things seem to be careening out of control, I remind myself of that heart-stopping "bump" in the air. Maybe that is why I like to compare marriage to flying.

One person famously associated with flight keeps coming to mind — Amelia Earhart. Her legend embodies many of the same elements we experience while navigating through the skies of marriage.

When she disappeared somewhere in the South Pacific on June 29, 1937 — while attempting to become the first woman to fly around the world — Earhart had already experienced success and satisfaction along with frustration and failure in her career. Her flying expeditions were not all smooth, but they were not all stormy either.

In the expansive and exciting skies of marriage, a smooth ride is hoped for but not realistic. Unforeseen navigational problems arise, dark clouds signal trouble, and conflicting flight patterns force us into "bumpy flights."

With God's help and wise instruction, however, we can avoid the hard knocks when the turbulence upsets the flight pattern. Some preparation and plenty of communication — along with checking and re-checking — can get husbands and wives from point A to point B without straying off course.

Sadly, however, especially when it comes to finances, many marriages crash shortly after takeoff. The most dangerous scenario, however, is not stormy weather or mechanical failure. Most marital crash landings occur when the pilot and co-pilot veer off in different directions — with the same plane!

HEADED IN OPPOSITE DIRECTIONS

Dave and Joan started a restaurant and built it into one of the most popular eating places in the city. Since he often worked late, and his wife stayed home with the kids, Dave had become bored and tired of the constant pressure.

"I've been thinking about putting my business up for sale," Dave told a friend, "but Joan would be against it. After all the years it took to make the restaurant a success, she finally feels financially secure."

One day the owner of the building that housed their restaurant came by. "I'm going to be tearing down the current building and replacing it with an office complex. I'm sorry to do this to you, but I can make more money renting out office space."

Dave and Joan were very understanding. "I guess we'll just have to find another building," Joan said, facing the reality of the situation.

Her husband, on the other hand, saw this as the perfect opportunity to begin a new life and career.

A few months later, Dave introduced himself to a new guy at the country club where he played golf, and they quickly became friends. Dave is the outgoing type who has never met a stranger.

As they talked, Dave learned that Tom was an antique dealer who had traveled all over the world buying and selling rare 16th to 18th century furniture.

"I have always enjoyed collecting antiques," Dave said and became very interested in Tom's business.

After a couple of weeks, Tom mentioned, "With all my money tied up in inventory, I need to raise more capital to keep the business going. In fact, I'm looking for investors and was wondering if you'd be interested in helping me financially until I'm able to make enough to support myself."

"I don't know," Dave replied.

Tom was quick to point out that the antique furniture business was a small yet profitable industry. "With the dollar amount it costs to buy the furniture, only a handful of people can afford to buy it," he explained.

Dave thought, *I am getting tired and bored with my business, and it would be tough to relocate the restaurant. This would be the perfect investment opportunity.*

"How much do you need?" Dave asked.

Tom eagerly replied, "Forty thousand would put me back on the road to buying and selling more antiques."

"I'll have to talk this over with Joan," Dave told him.

After hearing all the facts, Joan was opposed to investing money in such a small industry, especially when she heard they would have to put up $40,000.

"But we would be investing our money," her husband pointed out. "And with my help I believe Tom can make it big. Plus, if he did make it big, you and I will hit the jackpot!"

Each time Joan tried to share negatives, Dave would instantly cut her off with "Lighten up, everything is going to be just fine." This is not an uncommon response for someone with Dave's highly optimistic outlook on life — one that seldom takes time to consider any potential pitfalls.

"I don't know," she replied hesitantly. "Remember, we're going to need every extra dollar to relocate the restaurant."

Dave continued to push Joan without considering any of her

suggestions or listening to her reasons for caution. "If your dad hadn't loaned us the money to start our business, we would never have been able to go after our dream," he reminded her.

The lure of a big payoff seduced Dave into seeing himself ditch his cropduster existence and ease into a Lear jet streaking toward the good life. By ignoring Joan's sharp discernment, he was now piloting this baby all by himself.

Without an agreement between him and his wife, Dave went ahead with his plan. He used the equity from his home and cashed in his life insurance policy to get the $40,000 needed to put Tom into the antique business again.

"I can't believe you would mortgage our future for an antique salesman you've only known for a few months!" Joan shouted.

"If you don't go down to the bank and sign the papers, I will leave you," Dave threatened.

As so often happens in marriages, Dave had wrested control of the situation away from his wife and now had them headed for disaster. Joan, realizing that she was not going to be able to change her husband's mind, complied and signed the papers.

Shortly after, Dave and Tom joined together in the antique business. The $40,000 wasn't enough to keep the business afloat, however, and it plummeted like a rock. In addition to the devastating financial loss, Joan was left with deep anger and resentment toward her husband. Eventually, they divorced.

Dave and Joan had been headed in opposite directions without

THERE IS A BURDEN OF CARE IN GETTING RICHES; FEAR IN KEEPING THEM; TEMPTATION IN USING THEM; GUILT IN ABUSING THEM; SORROW IN LOWING THEM; AND A BURDEN OF ACCOUNT AT LAST TO BE GIVEN CONCERNING THEM.

MATTHEW HENRY (1662-1714)

even knowing it. If they had understood the differences in their temperaments and been aware of what each other needed, maybe their money conflict could have been avoided — and their marriage saved.

Understanding you and your mate's money personality will help you with the all-important *navigational* aspects of your marriage. My sincere goal is to help you and your spouse pilot your marriage through an uncertain future toward the same point on the map.

Remember, we all live with the uncertainties of foul weather and technical difficulties, but by planning ahead and staying focused on the same goals, you and your mate can ride above the turbulence together and into blue skies.

WHAT MAKES YOU TICK?

Why do some people jump right into the cockpit without thinking twice about the issues involved? On the other hand, why does it take other people a year to make a simple purchase?

I have discovered there are two types of people in this world. Here is a quick little test to find out into which category you fit:

• When you approach a swimming pool, do you run and jump in without testing the water? If that describes you, you are considered to be a *plunger,* an extrovert.

• Are you the type who sticks your big toe in and slowly works your way into the water? If so, you would be called a *wader* (those who wade), an introvert.

For some reason, waders typically marry plungers.

You see, plungers jump right in, often causing severe stress for the "wader" spouse. They splash the cold water of uncertainty all over the other marriage partner. Or, to put it another way, they are already airborne off the diving board while their mate is still creeping up the ladder.

The way you approach life — and money — has a lot to do with your inborn temperament. Let's define this rather illusive term.

God used 23 sets of chromosomes from each of your parents and wove them together to make you. If you have brown hair, you will have brown hair even if you dye it blonde. You cannot change what God made you to be.

If you are an extrovert, you will always be an extrovert. Even if you try to tone down your personality, you are always going to be outgoing and uninhibited. It's like an airplane engine constantly idling.

If you weigh every decision, look at the sidewalk when approaching someone, or carefully ration affection, you'll always be that way no matter how much you try to rev up your personality. It is simply your nature to sit on the tarmac and repeat safety checks from the cockpit.

Marriage brings together two unique individuals — each with a different temperament — into a relationship that only God could make. Authors Gary Smalley and John Trent, Ph.D., developed a test to help us determine our temperament type and included it in their book, *Two Sides of Love*. They have identified four different types and labeled them according to prototypes in the animal kingdom:

- Lions
- Otters
- Golden Retrievers
- Beavers[1]

This is a fun, but practical, way to identify unique traits and how they affect your marriage. Understanding your temperament enables you to identify your strengths and weaknesses as well as your mate's. This is important not only in the marriage relationship but also in how we handle money. These traits will either control your money, or you will learn to control the traits, thereby maintaining a handle on your financial situation. Even a cute otter or beaver can be capable of mischief and needs to be held in check.

Tim LaHaye, in the book *Smart Money*, which he co-authored with Jerry and Ramona Tuma, makes this statement: "Most Christians spend their lives far below their financial potential because they do not recognize their inherent financial weaknesses and do not practice God's principles for financially maximizing their potential."[2]

The Bible says, "God has given each of us the ability to do certain things well" (Rom. 12:6). Knowing your financial strengths will help you put your God-given abilities to work. We are to be responsible stewards of everything we are given.

As you read the characteristics of each temperament type, you will probably find yourself in one or more types. At the end of this section, I will share how different types blend together.

Understanding you and your mate's money personality will help you with the all-important *navigational* aspects of your marriage.

LIONS: TAKING THE LEAD

Lions tend to be great leaders because they are independent, decisive, powerful, and have great vision.

You can normally spot a lion at a relatively young age. He is the kid who recruits his buddies to work at his lemonade stand and then holds a training seminar on "How to Make Lemonade Faster" so they can serve more people — which, of course, means greater profits.

At a young age, lions already know the value of a dollar. Their brains have a natural profit-loss mechanism for developing great deals that will ultimately put money in their pockets. In short, lions are great entrepreneurs.

Lions are also oblivious to obstacles, hurdles, or fear. If their plan doesn't work one way, they will find another method to make it work. The lion's roar always makes the sound, "CAN DO!"

As soon as lions establish a goal, nothing can ground them. Like a laser beam cutting through a diamond, they become so focused — and make their efforts so concentrated — that they almost always reach their intended objective. This kind of intense focus keeps them extremely busy. Lions always have activities going and could even make work for a snow cone salesman in Siberia!

Money is very important to lions, and they use it as a measuring stick of success. As a result, they constantly compare themselves with other people and are often preoccupied with possessions and prestige. This obsession creates an endless push to get more — sometimes at the expense of other people. In fact, some lions can become so preoccupied with themselves and their own success that they easily trample other people without even seeing them.

Lions make great leaders. If they become consumed with one goal, however, they have a tendency to get their priorities out of balance.

TRAITS OF A LION

• *Lions are natural leaders.*

Think about the bosses you have worked for. You will probably notice that most of them exhibited a take-charge, bossy — and even pushy — personality.

Lions are also very self-reliant. In a marriage, it is not unusual for a lion to assume full responsibility of managing the family finances.

• *Lions are great visionaries.*

You've met these guys. They are the type who work for the sole purpose of retiring early. From the time they are little lion cubs, they have their goals written down on paper — even to the day each will be accomplished.

• *Lions are high risk takers.*

Once lions get into the vision zone, they start believing that anything is possible. Often over-confident, they think they can do it all and with their own abilities.

Lions need to count the cost before starting a project. The financial world is littered with the wrecks of lion ventures that hit quicksand because of poor planning.

• *Lions can have misplaced priorities.*

This makes them susceptible to finding their security in their work, possessions, prestige, and money. Lions can get hung up on their worldly treasures and use them to determine how well they are doing in life.

• *Lions are fast movers.*

When they find something they like or believe in, they will jump in with both feet. Lions are easily attracted to making a fast dollar and are often taken in by get-rich schemes.

• *Lions are very factual and practical.*

If a salesman can make a deal sound good and make sense, then lions are usually the first to buy. "Just the facts" is a motto most lions live by. If you live or work with a lion you will often find their hands making a motion telling you to get to the point.

• *Lions are self-sufficient.*

You will seldom find a lion down and out. They may be down for the count, but they will always re-surface. Lions make great entrepreneurs because they always learn from their past mistakes — which occur frequently.

• *Lions like to be challenged.*

An obstacle to a lion is like a protein shake. A challenge can bring instant energy into a lion. If you are having a hard time getting your finances figured out, give the project to a lion. He will take the project on with intensity and have it finished in a couple of hours.

• *Lions are decisive.*

When a decision needs to be made, ask a lion. He or she will know exactly what to do, how to do it, and what the outcome will be. Lions can seldom be labeled as indecisive.

My dad has a lot of lion in him. I think that's why I never remember a time when I felt insecure. No matter what obstacle we faced as a family, I knew that dad was going to take care of the problem. When my parents had to sell their business, my dad told us that changes had to be made and times ahead would be tough. Within two weeks we moved out of our house and into another one we could afford.

A lion can react quickly to situations. When you are in trouble, it pays to have a lion on your team.

From a financial standpoint, lions can be the "point man," taking the lead and avoiding money difficulties. Or, they can become so caught up in their own abilities that they make bad decisions. Lions need the balance of another personality type to keep them on course.

"GROUND CHECK" TIPS FOR LIONS

As a frequent "standby" passenger for many years, I was often bumped from flights and left to spend hours aimlessly wandering around airport terminals. To fill the down time, I often watched the planes preparing for take-off.

I noticed that the pilot and co-pilot would walk around their plane checking for any possible problems — low tires, loose bolts, and anything that could hamper a smooth flight. Once inside the cockpit they continued checking, pushing buttons, adjusting headsets, going over flight plans. Their thorough inspection never failed to impress me.

As a married couple, you and your co-pilot regularly need to complete a "ground check." Here is a suggested check list for the lion spouse:

1. Check your JOY gauge: Jesus first; Others second; Yourself third.

A lion can become so preoccupied with goals that he runs roughshod over his spouse without batting an eye. You need to regularly assess your attitude and ask yourself: Is Jesus first? Is my wife second? Remember, goals are short term, but relationships last a lifetime.

2. Make sure both pilot and co-pilot are seated at the controls.

For optimum efficiency and safety, both you and your spouse should have both hands on the throttle and an eye on the instrument panel. A lion will often operate in one of two ways: Either he will take complete control over the family finances or delegate the full responsibility to his mate (usually with a sink-or-swim attitude!). If, however, both partners are given equal input in financial decisions, conflict and frustration will be kept at a minimum — especially on a long flight!

3. Prepare for a slow, smooth take-off.

Most lions are determined to be millionaires before they reach puberty! With a knack for moving too fast and a passion to see immediate results, lions are susceptible to debt and greed. When a lion's spouse detects a high level of impatience in his or her mate, it is time to put on the brakes.

4. Select experienced crew members.

Lions need to surround themselves with a team of knowledgeable, wise, and godly advisors. Instead of barreling ahead at full throttle, take time to get sensible input on financial decisions that will affect your family's future.

OTTERS: LIFE OF THE PARTY

If you are having a party, invite an otter. Otters are parties waiting to happen. These extreme extroverts usually attract lots of attention — on purpose, of course. At your office, church, or club, he or she is usually the person surrounded by a group of happy people all listening to the otter.

Otters love to be in the spotlight. They love to be telling a joke or a good story. Having a good time is their main goal in life. If something is not fun to an otter, he will not take part and will be looking for another place to have fun.

My wife Kari is an off-the-chart otter. You will not find a more fun person in the entire world! (Okay, I'm a little biased.) When Kari walks into a room and flashes her brilliant smile, the whole place lights up. I always tell Kari, "If you had been a waitress, you would have made a killing!"

My temperament embodies some otter traits as well. This combination sometimes works against us. When we were dating, we shopped together a lot. "Isn't this cute, honey?" Kari would ask excitedly.

"That's great!" I'd shout. "Buy it!" After all, it was still *her* money. Then we would give each other a "high five" as the store clerks rolled their eyes. As we admired our latest purchases, we failed to realize that this kind of blind "take-off" would later end up a nose-dive in married life.

The otter's larger-than-life optimism, however, sometimes causes them to overlook the little details in life — like price tags.

After we were married, Kari and I took a trip to Bermuda. One day while we were eating in a little cafe, we noticed a young lady who resembled a famous television personality. Finally, I gathered up my courage and went over and introduced myself. "I can't believe how much you look like Connie Selleca," I told her.

"Who?" she asked. "I've never heard of her."

Her reply left me undaunted, and I proceeded (in fine otter fashion) to find out her true identity. She turned out to be an artist from Ireland who designed china.

Kari and I got to know her, and she invited us to come by the shop where she was displaying her china and signing autographs.

The next day, when we saw our friend's beautiful Irish design with shamrocks, Kari said, "Wouldn't it be a great idea to buy your mom a coffee cup and saucer?"

"Yeah!" I replied eagerly, knowing she collects coffee cups from all over the world. "It would really be special to have the actual designer autograph it." Kari picked out the cup and saucer and went to have our designer friend sign it. Then I proudly carried our treasure to the counter to pay for it. When the clerk totaled the cost, I almost fainted, "That will be $95.00."

Otters seldom check a price tag before they buy. That's why they are usually the ones gasping for breath at the checkout counter.

You may also have encountered an unashamed otter at the bank. He's the guy closing out his account because he never balances his checkbook and has no idea how much money he has left. If you follow him, he will go down the street to the next bank and open a new account. When that account gets messed up, he will repeat the process. Why does an otter's checkbook always look as if it has never been used? Because it hasn't! He always has a new one.

OTTER TRAITS

• *Otters are great salespeople.*

With their smiles and charisma, otters can make big money in sales. With their network of people, they could probably get into the White House if they really wanted to — and some of them have actually made it!

• *Otters are highly optimistic.*

Otters usually see positive before they see negative. At the office where I work, the majority of the staff have a lot of otter traits. My boss, on the other hand, has a more negative temperament.

As otters we never see or think of negatives until someone else brings it up. This kind of blind optimism makes otters susceptible to getting into debt.

Otters are plungers. They need to think about negatives because they can be burned (like our friend Dave) — if they are not careful.

• *Otters tend to be big givers.*

Otters love to put God to work in the faith category. Otters will give huge sums of money to universities and colleges so they can have a building or department named after them.

• *Otters are impulsive.*

If they see a good deal, otters will jump at the chance even if they don't need the item. (Remember my truck?) "Sale" — from 10 percent to 80 percent — is irresistible to an otter. They can't resist a bargain.

• *Otters prefer to skip the details.*

The otter's biggest hang-up is lack of attention to details. I love to come up with ideas, but I don't like to follow through with the nitty-gritty details.

Otters become easily bored. If a project is not entertaining, an otter will bail out in a flash. Financial meetings are very difficult for otters because of all the details that are involved.

• *Otters tend to be poor planners.*

Remember, otters live for the moment. The future is somewhere down the road, and today is much more fun.

The word "budget" sends chills up and down the otter's spine.

• *Otters are motivated by recognition.*

Praise is a great remedy to an otter. When an otter does balance — or even attempts to balance — a checkbook, you should reach for the pom-poms and call out the marching band. If you give him lots of praise, he might try it again.

"GROUND CHECK" TIPS FOR OTTERS

The otter's upbeat personality requires regular checkups to make sure he or she is on track. These points need special attention:

1. Idle before take-off.

Otters are notorious for spontaneous buying. If you are an otter, two steps will help you reduce impulse purchasing. First, set a limit for discretionary spending — like $20 or so. Any single item or

Your Money Personality

SOME HAVE MUCH, AND SOME HAVE MORE,

SOME ARE RICH, AND SOME ARE POOR,

SOME HAVE LITTLE,

SOME HAVE LESS

SOME HAVE NOT

A CENT TO BLESS;

THEIR EMPTY POCKETS,

YET POSSESS

TRUE RICHNESS IN TRUE HAPPINESS.

JOHN OXENHAM (1861–1941)

. . . .

expense over the determined amount requires the approval of your spouse. Second, allow 24 hours to pass before making any "over $20" purchase - even if your husband or wife considers it a great deal. Many times, that new sofa or chain saw doesn't seem as necessary — or as appealing — the next day.

2. Keep your hands on the throttle.

In the case of the otter shopper: Keep your hands in your pockets! Fun, fun, fun — that's why an otter goes shopping. It's an adventure! Forget the sightseeing; take her to the gift shop! For my wife Kari, "going shopping" means just that! No pointless window browsing for her. To go to the mall and not buy something is like sitting in front of the TV without turning it on — boring. Otters need to make "self-control" their motto.

3. Check your flight plan often.

By planning, otters can eliminate 90 percent of their money chaos. Since otters tend to live for the moment, preparing for the future never enters their minds. Predetermined goals help keep the otter on course and eliminates the partner's frustration and anger over side-tracked spending.

4. Consult your co-pilot.

Of the four temperaments, otters find money management most difficult — not because they can't do it but because it's not "fun."

Nothing is more agonizing to an otter than balancing a checkbook or planning for retirement. Proper money management, however, cannot be neglected. To be a responsible steward, you need to solicit the help of your mate and make yourself accountable to him or her — and to God — when it comes to money.

GOLDEN RETRIEVER: A NICE GUY

Everybody loves a golden retriever. They are beautiful, obedient, loving, and loyal dogs. If you are looking to buy a dog and want to research which breed would be best for your family, the golden retriever tops many recommended lists.

Barney Fife from "The Andy Griffith Show" portrays a model golden retriever. In one episode, Barney bought a used car from an elderly lady who told him, "My husband passed away, and I only drove the car to Thursday night bingo."

Barney, who tends to be the softy but tries to act like a big man, immediately agreed to buy the car. Andy gets suspicious and has the car checked by his faithful mechanic, Goober. They realize that the little old lady is trying to pull one over on Barney.

Good old Barney finds it hard to believe that anyone so sweet could be so deceptive. Like the typical golden retriever, he believes the best about everybody.

In many ways, the traits of the golden retrievers are almost diametrically opposed to those of the lion and otter.

TRAITS OF A GOLDEN RETRIEVER

• *Golden retrievers are good planners.*

Golden retrievers can plan, plan, and plan. Believe it or not, golden retrievers are good analyzers, so they can take a bad situation — such as their finances — find out where the problem is, and come up with a great plan to turn financial chaos into easy street.

• *Golden retrievers tend to procrastinate.*

This is the number one hindrance of a golden retriever. They can make plans until they are blue in the face, but the major setback is that they never get around to putting the plan into action.

The Nike phrase: "Just Do It" needs to be the golden retriever's motto. A friend of mine, Michelle, is a typical retriever. She never opens bills, and you can fast forward to see where this gets her!

• *Golden retrievers are savers.*

A major need of golden retrievers is security. It is not unusual for them to have lots of money in their checking account just in case something happens.

"The money will come in handy," the retriever tells his spouse while she is forced to skimp on groceries and necessities.

• *Golden retrievers can be low-risk takers.*

Because of their need for security, golden retrievers tend to avoid any form of uncertainty. There is nothing wrong with minimizing your risk, but when it comes to finances and you are young, a little risk can take you a long way.

• *Golden retrievers cultivate deep friendships.*

A golden retriever normally has one or two best friends. Why? Because they tend to go very deep and have long conversations, they never get around to talking to other people.

• *Golden retrievers have plenty of patience.*

You can always spot a golden retriever by how he or she quietly stands in line. They don't roll their eyes, give dirty looks, or glance at their watch every ten seconds to let everyone know how busy they are. They know they can't do anything about it, so why worry?

• *Golden retrievers like to avoid conflicts.*

Golden retrievers will go out of their way to make sure no conflicts occur, even if it means that they will be trampled on in the process. They will bend over backwards, walk the tightrope, or dig a hole to the other side of the earth to avoid conflict.

• *Golden retrievers are memory keepers.*

If you are married to one, you know what I mean. Kari has many golden retriever traits, and she considers any item linked to a special event a treasure.

When I played football in high school, I sprained my big toe (don't ask me how I did it). The team trainer taped my big toe to my other toe so I could continue to play. After the game, my big toe had swelled up to the size of a cantaloupe. When I took the tape off, my big toenail came off with it. Kari happened to be present for this "bonding moment," so she took the toenail and put it in her memory box without my knowing it.

A few years later as we were going through her memory box, we came across this very gross object. When I asked her, "What is this?" Kari replied, "Do you remember in high school when you injured your toe?" I couldn't believe it! Now *that* is a "memory keeper."

"GROUND CHECK" TIPS FOR GOLDEN RETRIEVERS

Imagine if one of these low-key, lovable characters owned an airline. He would probably let everyone fly free — but the planes would never get off the ground! That's why the golden retriever's check points are much different from those required for the lion and otter.

1. Just say, "NO!"

Retrievers are a salesman's dream. They will do anything to avoid hurting anyone's feelings. Have you ever heard a golden retriever on the phone with a telemarketer? "A service plan for my toaster oven? Why sure, deary. Just sign me up. I know you're only trying to make a living. It was so nice of you to call." Retrievers need to stand in front of the mirror and practice saying, "No!"

2. Learn to hang-glide.

Golden retrievers must "let go" of their security blankets and trust God to meet their needs. Once they see the results of faithfully giving their money to further God's kingdom, they often become the most faithful tithers and loyal givers.

3. Face the winds head on.

That means: Open all the bills as soon as you get them. With their tendency to procrastinate, golden retrievers should put their planning skills to work in this area of money management. At least once a month, set aside two hours on a specific day to pay all the bills and balance your checkbook.

4. Put a bomb on board!

The number one complaint of retriever spouses is: "I have to put a bomb under my husband just to get him moving!" If you are a slow mover, I suggest you enlist the help of your spouse. Ask him or her to set time limits on money-management projects like: All ATM receipts must be turned in by the 15th of the month — or your card is confiscated!

BEAVER: THE BEST OF EVERYTHING

My brother in-law Randy, is a model beaver. When I was younger, Randy used to take me fishing for rainbow trout up in the White Mountains of Arizona. On our first trip, Randy took me to a creek so crystal clear I could see the fish swimming in the water. As an inexperienced fisherman, I cast my line right on top of the fish, not knowing I was supposed to bring the lure to them.

Randy taught me all the tricks of an expert fisherman. (Thanks,

Randy, for putting up with me for all these years. Sorry for losing all your lures.) Randy always had the right equipment with him. If the water was muddy, he had a special lure. If the fish were down deep in the water, he had another lure to catch them. If it was morning or evening, he had the right lures. A beaver is usually prepared for the unexpected.

Beavers make the best shoppers in the household and the best dressers at work. Their homes have the nicest appliances, their cars have state-of-the-art stereo systems, and their garages contain the latest sporting equipment — all neatly organized, of course.

TRAITS OF A BEAVER

• *Beavers are good organizers.*

They always have a "right" place to put everything. A beaver is great around a file cabinet. When tax season rolls around they are always first to get their taxes into the IRS because they are the only ones who can find their papers.

• *Beavers have "great taste."*

Beavers know their stuff. Whether stereo equipment, clothes, or cars, beavers tend to know where and how to buy the best.

• *Beavers are perfectionists.*

Every beaver has a subscription to *Consumer Reports.* Before a beaver buys an item, he will spend hours researching to find the highest quality brand at the best price.

• *Beavers have discernment.*

Beavers have the ability to determine a good financial investment from a bad one. With all the opportunities available today, this kind of wisdom is crucial.

• *Beavers crave schedules.*

A "day-timer" or other daily notebook organizer is essential to beavers. They love to plan and organize their commitments and schedules on paper. Companies will spend thousands of dollars to send their employees to organizing seminars, so they can learn what comes naturally to a beaver.

• *Beavers tend to be reserved.*

Beavers do not show a lot of emotions. In tough times, they are able to function effectively without allowing their emotions to distract them from the situation at hand.

• *Beavers can be controlling.*

Because of their organizational skills, beavers can become very controlling. If one spouse is a beaver, he or she is usually the family money manager. The beaver, however, needs to be careful not to be overly dictatorial about how the money is spent.

"GROUND CHECK" TIPS FOR BEAVERS

Of the four temperaments, managing finances comes most naturally to the beaver because he loves detail. This guy (or gal) is such a perfectionist that only one way is the right way — his way! His check list is simple.

1. Forget the checklist!

No one expects you to be perfect — except you! Learn to say, "I'm sorry." If you will admit your mistakes (granted they are few and far between) you will eliminate unwanted arguments and keep your spouse from breaking all your lead pencils.

2. Listen to your co-pilot.

Believe it or not, your way is not always the best way! Take time to consider your spouse's suggestions. When dealing with your mate on financial issues, remind yourself that less than perfection is okay. You are a team. Remember, it's only money!

3. Learn to coast.

You need to sit back and enjoy the ride. Take the pressure off yourself. Forget about having the perfect budget, the best investment portfolio, or the most organized system. After all, who cares?

4. Take a back seat.

Put God in the pilot's seat, and let Him be in full control. Let go, and let God put on the captain's hat. You may be surprised to learn that He can solve problems in a moment that would take you years to figure out. Learn to depend on Him and godly counselors for wisdom.

BUDGETING BY TEMPERAMENT

Let's look at how each of the different temperaments would attack putting a budget together.

A lion would call his CPA: "Hey, Bob, I know you're busy but could you put together a budget for me? I'll come by tomorrow and pick it up at noon."

An otter would allot some money for the basic expenses — like rent, car payment, utilities — but most of his spending would be concentrated on entertainment, luncheons, gym memberships, and anything else that adds fun to his life.

A golden retriever would think about the budget for awhile. Then when his wife finally demands one, he will put one together.

Of the four temperaments, the beaver will probably make the most detailed list of income and expenses down to the last penny. Beavers are great planners and organizers. Financial management comes more naturally to the beaver than other types.

Beavers are often chief financial officers, treasurers, accountants, etc. Beavers can be very critical not only of themselves but also of others. With their need for perfection, anything less is considered a loss.

If you are a beaver and your mate is not recording checks accurately or sticking to the budget as planned, you are probably very frustrated. After all, your world is out of order.

I know beavers who budget a can of soda once a week for themselves at work. Their strength of being alert to details can actually become a weakness if it is pushed too far.

When a beaver is married to an otter, both are probably very frustrated. The weaknesses of one mate are the other's strengths — and neither can understand their differences.

TEMPERAMENT COMBINATIONS

Most people have more then one dominant temperament. Even though we all have some characteristics of all four temperaments, the second major temperament will be more evident than the two remaining.

Lion/Beaver.

This is a take-charge, organized person — the ultimate manager. He or she likes things to be right and done quickly. I should have taken a lion-beaver with me when I went back to the car dealership to exchange my new truck. He would have researched all my options and accessed the best information to get the best result.

In a marriage these traits have positive and negative consequences. The lion/beaver can become so consumed with a project the other mate feels left out. This is also true when it comes to decision-making, which is usually one-sided. This high-powered personality tends to take over and not seek input from his or her mate.

Otter/Lion.

The ultimate optimist, the otter/lion is forever dreaming of what can happen next. He has the potential to be a big spender. Remember restaurateurs Dave and Joan? Dave is a perfect example of an otter/lion.

These people need to be wary of assuming too much debt. Business opportunities and the pursuit of acquiring fun possessions can easily put them into the hole. Potentially, they can become great givers since they are high-risk takers.

Golden Retriever/Otter.

These individuals have the potential to earn lots of money. They can become great sales people. With the charm of an otter and ability to read into individuals, they can cater to any client's needs.

With the ability to earn big dollars, they can also lose big dollars. Their expensive taste and poor record-keeping ability, however, could result in financial disaster if not controlled.

Having a good time is the name of their game.

Beaver/Golden Retriever.

This is the ultimate "Consumer Report" junkie. Before making a major purchase, this person will do research and more research.

They can also be very fear-driven. Security is very important to them, making them very low-risk takers.

We could go on and on listing different temperament combinations and how they relate to finances, but you probably get the idea.

SETTING THE STAGE FOR CHANGE

Why is it important to know your temperament and that of your spouse? So you can identify your strengths and weaknesses. This enables you and your mate to distribute your talents to maximize your efforts at managing your money — and your marriage.

Throughout this chapter, you were probably thrilled to discover strengths you did not know you had. Now you must make a conscious effort to use your strengths to improve your financial situation.

One word of caution: If you push your strengths too far, they can overwhelm your spouse and create even greater conflict. For example, the over-organized beaver can suffocate his partner with details and take all the joy and creativity out of planning a budget together — or making other financial decisions.

Being aware of your weaknesses and how they can trigger potential conflict with your mate merely sets the stage for change. Keep

YOUR MONEY PERSONALITY

Personality Profile

In the space provided, identify the degree to which the following characteristics or behaviors most accurately describe you.

0 = not at all; 1 = somewhat; 2 = mostly; 3 = very much

I	II	III	IV
__Likes control	__Enthusiastic	__Sensitive	__Consistent
__Confident	__Visionary	__Calm	__Reserved
__Firm	__Energetic	__Non-demanding	__Practical
__Likes challenge	__Promoter	__Enjoys routine	__Factual
__Problem solver	__Mixes easily	__Relational	__Perfectionist
__Bold	__Fun-loving	__Adaptable	__Detailed
__Goal-driven	__Spontaneous	__Thoughtful	__Inquisitive
__Strong-willed	__Likes new ideas	__Patient	__Persistent
__Self-reliant	__Optimistic	__Good listener	__Sensitive
__Persistent	__Takes risks	__Loyal	__Accurate
__Takes charge	__Motivator	__Even-keeled	__Controlled
__Determined	__Very verbal	__Gives in	__Predictable
__Enterprising	__Friendly	__Indecisive	__Orderly
__Competitive	__Popular	__Dislikes change	__Conscientious
__Productive	__Enjoys variety	__Dry humor	__Discerning
__Purposeful	__Group oriented	__Sympathetic	__Analytical
__Adventurous	__Initiator	__Nurturing	__Precise
__Independent	__Inspirational	__Tolerant	__Scheduled
__Action oriented	__Likes change	__Peace maker	__Deliberate
____Total	____Total	____Total	____Total

Record your totals in the appropriate areas on the graph below.

	I	II	III	IV
60				
50				
40				
30				
20				
10				
0				
	I=L	II=O	III=GR	IV=B

in mind that change happens from the inside out. Instead of focusing on your mate's weaknesses, start to work on improving those areas in your own life that are undermining your financial stability — and affecting your marriage.

It has been said that "knowledge is power." That is true to a point. Knowledge of our strengths and weaknesses, however, only has value if we acknowledge our weaknesses and ask God to help us to improve in those areas.

Change is a process that takes time. Keep in mind that we are on a journey. And a journey not only has a present and future, it also has a past — all our yesterdays.

At times, our strengths can become weaknesses because of the way our past has shaped our attitudes about money.

• Are you often suspicious about what your mate is doing with money?

• Do you spend money that you know you don't have?

• When you are around other people, do you feel guilty that you have more money than you need? Or are you ashamed about your less-than-prosperous financial state?

In the next chapter, we will explore how our past has helped shape our spending habits and the way we feel about money.

CHAPTER THREE
YOUR MONEY PAST

A FEW years ago, when Kari and I moved from Phoenix to Branson, Missouri, we had expected to purchase a house and settle quickly into country living. We had not taken into account, however, that Branson was a "boom town" filled with country-western shows and other forms of family entertainment. People were moving in from everywhere!

As we began to house hunt, it became clear that few homes were on the market — and those available were highly overpriced. Our only alternative was to build a house. Eventually, we found property out in the country and put up stakes — surveyor stakes!

After drawing up plans and retaining a reasonably-priced builder, Kari and I forked over our savings.

During the initial construction stages, Kari mentioned — ever so sweetly, I might add — "Wouldn't it be nice to have a separate dining area where we could have big family dinners — especially at the holidays?"

"Well . . ." I hesitated, knowing the extra footage would add significantly to the base price we had agreed upon. "I guess we need it," was my reluctant answer.

As with most building projects, other unexpected "extras" also crept in, and — before we knew it — we were way over budget.

"What are we going to do?" I mumbled while staring at the builder's latest invoice.

Kari — who was thrilled with the way the house was progressing — seemed oblivious to our dilemma. Her attention was focused on selecting lighting fixtures and drapery fabric.

"Looks like I'll have to go back to the bank and increase the amount of our loan," I said, hoping to jolt her back to reality.

"Oh, well . . ." she remarked, apparently unconcerned about what I perceived to be a very serious obligation. "I can't wait 'til the house is finished!"

Moving day finally arrived.

Thrilled to get settled in our brand new home, we eagerly arranged all our furniture and got everything put in its proper place. That's when we noticed this big blank area: A giant, empty cavern with no furnishing — the dining room!

"When can we go shopping for a dining room table?" Kari asked immediately.

Knowing our reserve funds were depleted, I hesitantly replied, "We'll have to wait awhile."

"Why?"

"Don't you remember the big check we just wrote to the builder for all the extras on the house?"

"Oh, yeah. . . ." Kari's face said it all — the party's over!

Not wanting to rain on her parade, I quickly added, "But we'll get one soon."

Months passed.

"When are we going to buy a dining room table?" Kari began to ask more insistently. I could tell she was agitated with me. (Men can sense these things.)

"When we get the money!" I shot back.

As time went on, we eventually turned the dining room into a playroom for Michael and Hannah.

After a year of my saying, "Soon, honey," Kari finally asked: "Just what is your definition of *soon?*"

I could not answer her. In fact, I had no idea why I was waiting.

The "soon" comment, however, precipitated many other arguments.

"Look," she said one day, "we have been saving consistently for more than a year to build up our savings. Surely we can afford to buy a dining room table!"

"Not yet!" I replied angrily.

After my truck fiasco, we had learned the importance of being in agreement before making a major purchase. This time, however, I was the one holding out.

After all, I thought, *how important is a dining room table that will only be used a few times a year?* It wasn't until later that I understood the true reason for my reluctance.

Kari and I did not realize that events in our pasts were affecting not only our present attitudes about money but our decisions about how and when to spend it.

We all have fond memories — *and* painful ones. Events and attitudes — both good and bad — shape us and affect how we react in differing circumstances.

When confronting my own money past, I sometimes shudder to remember the experiences that shaped me. (More on that in a minute.)

BACK TO THE FUTURE

Do you remember your first encounter with money? Was it happy, painful, or embarrassing?

It could have been at the grocery store when you wanted a candy bar, but your mom said, "I don't have enough money for that today."

Maybe it was that toy every other kid owned, but that your parents could not afford to buy. Or maybe your parents stretched their budget to keep up with the neighbors and their kids.

At some point, you may have heard your parents arguing about money. On the other hand, maybe money issues were never discussed in the open.

As a teenager, you may have rammed the family car into the garage. Did your dad ask, "How are you going to pay for this?" or merely reply, "Don't worry about it"?

When I look back on my own financial shaping, I recall two very distinct events in my own life. One was my first encounter with money, and the second was my first encounter with money in relationship to love and acceptance from the opposite sex.

I first noticed the importance of money when I was about five years old.

My dad, who was a pastor in southern California at the time, was called by God to move to a church in northern California. At the going away party, the church members prepared a farewell gift. When they presented the gift to our family, they gave it to me.

Like any normal five year old holding a present, I proceeded to tear open the gift. To my delight inside the box was a miniature moving van. I instantly thanked everyone and went off to play with my new toy.

As I opened the back of the tiny trunk, a stack of green paper fell to the floor. Before I could pick it up, my dad stuffed the large roll in his pocket. I learned later that the green paper was a love offering to help us through our transition to the new church.

From that point on, I began to understand that this "green paper" was very important and not to be treated lightly.

All of us have money events in our past that have molded the way we handle finances. These kinds of events:

• Have an impact on our financial outlook.
• Affect the choices we make.
• Determine how we manage our personal and family finances.

When events concerning money — like the ones described above — occur, they are seldom dealt with openly by parents.

DEATH, SEX, AND MONEY

They say the hardest subjects to talk about are death and sex. I think money should also be included in that list.

I am often approached by people who want to discuss their financial situation with me. If another person comes close enough to hear our conversation, the person I am counseling will change the subject. No one wants to admit — or let others know — they have money problems. The subject of money is hush-hush, especially when it becomes too personal.

One of the most delicate situations between an engaged couple occurs when one of them asks the bombshell question: "How much money do you make?" Unless this is handled properly, one party may feel threatened or become resentful.

For the same reason, employers do not post employees' salaries for all to see, nor do workers stand around the water and say, "Guess how much money I make!"

The same kind of secrecy occurs in families. Over the years, children — both rich and poor — develop misconceptions about financial obligations because the subject is never openly discussed. As a result, young adults fail to approach money realistically. Instead, they regard money as this ethereal, intangible substance that has no beginning or end.

Where do money problems begin? With the amount we have in the bank? No. Problems with money begin in the mind. Events in our past shape our current perception of money.

Jan grew up in a working class home where her father "ruled the roost." With five mouths to feed, her parents had little left over for extras. After earning a full scholarship to a local university, Jan graduated with honors and went on to earn her master's degree as an educational guidance counselor.

When her mother died, Jan felt responsible for her younger siblings and made sure they all had the opportunity to attend college. Finally, she married in her late twenties and had three children.

Jan continued to work, often saying, "I want my kids to have everything I didn't get growing up."

With two incomes, Jan and her husband made sure their children had designer label clothes, the latest Nintendo games, music lessons, sports equipment, and, of course, an "all-expenses-paid" college education.

"I know how I had to struggle — working and going to school," Jan would tell her husband when he complained about the mounting bills, "and I don't want my kids to go through that."

Peter, the eldest boy, has been going to college for nearly four years now. How do you think he handles money? He doesn't handle it for long, that's for sure.

As soon as he gets cash from dad, it's gone to pay for pizza or football tickets. Things that don't require cash are easily charged on his credit cards. "I'll pay those off when I get a great job," he tells his parents who worry about the debt he is assuming.

The only problem is: Graduation keeps getting pushed further and further into the future. "I think Peter will probably graduate next December if he doesn't change majors again," his mother reports. "At least he's enjoying his college years."

"Yeah, and I'm paying for it!" Dad laments.

The way we handle money today is determined long before we start a career or get married. As a result, it is difficult to unravel the events in our past that have contributed to the way we think, feel, manage, and spend money. We may, however, be able to identify a common thread that holds the key to our money past.

Your parents may have never talked openly about money. Or, maybe you had some bad experiences with money that cause you to feel uncomfortable whenever the subject comes up. Now, as an adult, you still feel uneasy discussing your personal finances with anyone — including your mate.

CINDERELLA AND PRINCE CHARMING

When I was in fifth grade, our family moved from California to Phoenix. Although my dad continued to serve the Lord, he left the pastorate and started his own business.

During high school, I was offered the opportunity to attend a private academy — which I eagerly accepted. Most of my classmates, of course, came from well-to-do families where "money was no object."

My first year, I had a crush on the prettiest girl in the class.

One day I happened to overhear her tell a friend, "A good-looking guy with an okay car is just average, but an okay-looking guy in a great-looking car is even better."

I didn't even own a car — much less a "great-looking" one. To make matters worse, most of the kids at my school received a new sports car on their 16th birthday.

That girl's comment changed my outlook on dating and affected my relationships for years to come. From that time on, I decided, "If I want to be considered good-looking, I need a great-looking car."

For the first time in my life, I began to associate love and acceptance with money and possessions.

Do you remember the first time you saw the movie *Cinderella?* In this adorable tale, a poor little girl lives with her wicked stepmother and mean step-sisters who force her to do all the housework. In the end, however, Cinderella wins the big prize and lives happily ever after with the handsome and rich prince.

It is no coincidence that the prince is very wealthy. I am not saying that money is evil or that being rich is bad, but the message is clear.

When, as young children, we start noticing what's going on around us, we learn that the world sells love, happiness, power, prestige, freedom, security, pleasure, fulfillment, and independence through money and possessions.

As we grow older, the message only gets more powerful: If you want to be loved and accepted, be sure you wear the right clothes, drive the right car, and have lots of money to spend. Then you'll be happy.

From Doris Day to Demi Moore, Hollywood continually promotes the conception that "diamonds are a girl's best friend" and "I'm worth it!" The message? Women prefer a man who can shower her with jewelry and surround her with mink. Of course, in the mov-

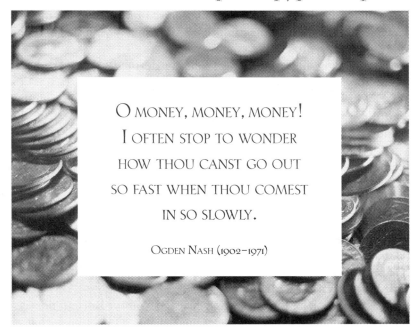

O MONEY, MONEY, MONEY!
I OFTEN STOP TO WONDER
HOW THOU CANST GO OUT
SO FAST WHEN THOU COMEST
IN SO SLOWLY.

OGDEN NASH (1902–1971)

ies, the rich men are always good-looking *and* rich — like Mel Gibson, Robert Redford, and Prince Charming.

This image puts tremendous pressure on us guys not only to provide financially for our wives but also to be able to lavish them with expensive gifts. As a result, some men try to communicate their love through material possessions.

"Diamonds are forever," the commercial softly whispers. In other words, if your wife doesn't have a diamond for every wedding anniversary, then you apparently don't love her.

Little girls are told by their mothers, "Marry rich!"

What do little boys think when they hear that message? That they need lots of money in order to find and keep a woman.

Maybe you have heard the comment, "When the money stops coming in the door, the love starts going out the window."

Television sitcoms and comedians constantly foster the idea that money is the binding force in a love relationship.

One joke is told of a father who snapped at his three-year-old son, "Get that quarter out of your mouth, there are germs on it." The wife then tells the little boy, "Don't worry, Jimmy, keep the quarter in your mouth. Even germs can't live on the money your dad makes."

In other words: Love equals *money!*

Whatever happened to love being defined as commitment, honor, or "for richer or poorer"?

When an individual's self-esteem and love are tied to money and possessions, selfishness and greed will eventually destroy the relationship. No wonder so many marriages end in divorce.

It was this subtle but powerful message equating love with money that led to the "great truck fiasco" early in my marriage to Kari.

CAN MONEY BUY HAPPINESS?

In a recent *Forbes* magazine article titled, "Does Money Buy Happiness?" the author explains his scientific approach to happiness. He conducted an extensive study of the world's wealthiest people from the "Forbes Four Hundred" list.

In this article, the author interviewed Warren Buffett, the second richest man in the United States, and asked, "Does money change people?"

Buffett answered, "Yes. If you were a jerk before, you'll be a bigger jerk with a billion dollars."[1]

In other words, money has nothing to do with your character, your personality, or your impact on society and mankind. Most of all, money cannot make you happy.

In his book, *1001 Great Stories and Quotes,* author R. Kent Hughes writes about Elvis Presley, who owned three jet airplanes, two Cadillacs, a Rolls-Royce, a Lincoln Continental, a Jeep, a dune buggy, three motorcycles — and several other vehicles.

His favorite car, a 1960 Cadillac limousine, had been sprayed with 40 coats of a specially prepared paint that included crushed diamonds. Most of the car's metal trim was plated with 18-karat gold. Inside the limo, Elvis had access to a gold-plated television, a gold electric razor and hair clippers, a refrigerator, and gold telephones.

Elvis seemed to have everything.

One day when he had a cold, one of Elvis' managers found him in the music room playing the hymn, "How Great Thou Art," on the piano.

"How do you feel?" the manager asked.

"Alone," was Presley's only response.

Elvis was rich outwardly, but poor within. Why? Because happiness cannot be bought; it can only be given away.

The magazine *InStyle* displays the hottest new styles and shows how movie stars decorate their homes. A full-page ad in this publication presents a picture of three generations of women — a grandmother, mom, and daughter — sitting in the back seat of a taxi blowing bubbles and smiling.

What are they selling? Bubble blowers? Would you believe — a wrist watch?

The ad, however, has nothing to do with the quality or function of this name-brand watch. In fact, we do not see any of the women even wearing a watch. What are the advertisers trying to do? To get you to buy the watch not because of its quality but because it will (supposedly) bring you great happiness.

What is the advertising industry's best marketing tool? To effectively communicate that if you buy their product, your life will be happy and fulfilled. Their perfume or soft drink or car will bring you prestige and power — and love.

While this may seem sinister on the part of the advertisers, it's actually just a fact of life. They know that "happiness" is everyone's goal in life, so they use it to sell their products.

If you watch a Burger King commercial, you may notice that the ads don't say anything about their burgers. Instead the message is: If you come to Burger King, you will be happy. All the happy people eat at Burger King.

I admit that a good burger will make me happy, but it is not the reason for my happiness.

The media bombards us with mixed money messages. Every day we are assaulted with TV commercials, magazine ads — and even our friends — telling us how they have found happiness in the latest electronic gadget or the newest exercise equipment or the current fashion trend.

All of us are influenced by what the world tells us we need to be fulfilled in life. Sometimes we set our sights on an expensive car, trendy furniture, or a bigger, better house in an effort to keep in step with our friends and relatives.

"Did you notice Barb's new leather sofa?" Ann mentioned to Jack as they drove away from her sister's home. "Wasn't it luxurious? And that bracelet she was wearing must have cost Sam a fortune!"

Jack braces himself for the latest blast.

"I'm the oldest. It's not fair that my younger sister is better off than I am!" Ann shot at her husband. "If you had a better-paying job we could afford to live the way they do!"

Although Ann and Jack owned a lovely home in a nice neighborhood, their lifestyle seemed tawdry compared to her sisters' affluence.

In an effort to keep up, Ann always had to buy "the best." It didn't matter if a cheaper brand of furniture or clothing was perfectly adequate, she would excuse her purchases with, "I just have expensive taste."

Frustrated over his wife's spending habits and demeaned by her constant ridicule of his job, Jack eventually withdrew — to the point where they no longer slept in the same room.

"I'm so lonely," Ann whined to her best friend. "We can't communicate anymore. If Jack really cared about me and the kids, he'd work harder to provide for us."

Ann put her marriage — and her own happiness — in jeopardy because she bought into the lie: Things make you happy.

At some point, we need to stop, re-evaluate our motives, and ask ourselves: Are "things" more important than people? Am I using "things" to fill a void in my life for prestige or acceptance? What will it take to make me content? When will enough be enough?

In a later chapter I will share how we can stop using possessions to meet our desire for the approval of others.

DEFINING YOUR FINANCIAL BACKGROUND

How would you define your financial background? To answer that question, you first have to ask yourself: How did my parents view money when I was growing up?

Think back to how your parents handled their finances. What positive principles did you learn from them?

Your parents may have given generously (and continue to do so) to the church. If so, they probably encouraged you at an early age to tithe and give offerings.

Without knowing it, you may have assimilated many positive traits from your parents' spending and saving habits. Or, you may have picked up a few negative tendencies that have followed you into your marriage relationship.

If a child comes from a home where no love was shown in the

family, he will not know how to love his own wife and children. The same principle applies to money. If the proper use of money was not taught or communicated to you in accordance with God's principles, you will not know how to give and save — nor be able to live financially free from spending and debt.

This is not the time to blame Mom and Dad because you have messed up your finances. Although your parents may have neglected to teach you the proper way to manage your finances, you can probably credit them with teaching you — as mine did — one crucial lesson: The value of hard work and the importance of earning an honest living.

As a teen, I thought day and night about having a Mustang GT convertible.

"Okay," my parents agreed, "but you have to earn the money to pay for it."

"Great!" I responded.

The job I got entailed using a jackhammer to remove old sidewalks. If you have ever visited the Phoenix area in July, you know the meaning of "sweltering heat." Compound that with operating a jackhammer, and you have the job from. . . . Well, let's just say, it was hot as blazes!

After a few days, my dreams of a Mustang had lost some appeal. A week later, my expectations of owning a hot car had been reduced to a more manageable level, and I quit my job. In a "concrete way," I learned the value of a dollar.

Thinking back to your past when you were 5, 7, or 18, do any money memories come up that you remember most? There may be two or three that keep returning that may have had a major impact on your "money shape." Take a few moments and think back to money events in your childhood and teenage years. Below is a list of questions to help you with this process.

- Were "money fights" frequent in your home?
- Did you often find yourself embarrassed to show your friends where you lived, having maybe a nicer home or a smaller home than your friends?
- Did you ever find yourself being ashamed of what you had? (Your parents had lots or little money?)
- Did you often daydream about having really nice things, so you could impress others?

- What was your first introduction to money?
- For your birthday or Christmas did you have lots of presents? One big expensive present? Cash inside your cards?
- What disadvantages did you experience being rich, middle class, or poor?
- What did your parents teach you about money? Spending and saving?
- When growing up did people tell you to find a rich spouse so you could live happily ever after?
- Did you get more or less of an allowance than your friends?
- What do you remember about getting your first paycheck? What did you do with your first paycheck?
- Did you ever say to yourself, "I can't wait until I get out on my own so I can do whatever I want"?
- Were your parents fair with their gifts, allowances, or purchases with all your siblings?
- Did you ever steal money from a piggy bank, parents, friends, etc.?
- Do you remember the first gift you ever gave to a church or a person in need?
- Were you rewarded for being good by receiving money or some kind of gift?

IDENTIFYING YOUR MONEY HABITS

In this section, you will be able to identify any inherited negative money habits.

Why have we focused most on the negative influences from our past? Because that is usually where change needs to begin. These same traits, however, also have an "up" side as you will see.

Let's look at the four primary traits that hinder healthy financial habits:

1. Over-spending.
2. Obsessive saving.
3. Using money to control your mate.
4. Giving to seek approval.

1. Over-spending.

Some people take a path opposite to the one traveled by their parents. Maybe your mom and dad were obsessive savers and insisted that everything you made from delivering newspapers, babysitting, or your allowance had to put in a savings account or a piggy bank. Now, as an adult, you spend everything you make on clothes, cars, or eating out because you don't want to be like your parents.

On the other hand, if your parents assumed large amounts of debt, you may have presumed, "This is how everybody lives." Now, you frequently borrow money to pay for the things you cannot afford.

Over-spending can also be triggered by an emotional need.

Jill's dad was an alcoholic who often erupted into violent rages. The day after one of his abusive rampages, he would say, "Come on. Let's go to the mall!" and buy her expensive gifts as a way of appeasing his conscience.

As a grown woman, Jill now goes on a shopping spree whenever she feels stressed out or depressed. In fact, her bumper sticker reads, "When the going gets tough, the tough go shopping!" Jill does not realize that her problem is no laughing matter. Uncontrolled, emotional spending will eventually take its toll not only financially but in every area of her life — especially her marriage.

If you like to shop, that can actually work to your advantage. A wise shopper can be a tremendous asset when it comes to getting to the "biggest bang for a buck." Wives are most often blessed with this gift. Like a private investigator, they can comb newspaper ads for sales, research out the best prices, and go after their intended target.

In the back of their minds, many women keep a running list of the particular needs of each family member. Then when sneakers — or dress shirts or underwear — go on sale, they move in for the kill. It's not unusual for a wise shopper to save 50 to 75 percent on sale items.

Being a spender can either work for you or against you; it's how and why you spend that determines the outcome. Whenever you have the urge to shop, ask yourself: Why am I going shopping? Is it for a particular need? Or simply to satisfy some emotional void in my life? The answer will pinpoint your true motivation.

2. Obsessive saving.

Unlike the spender, you may have promised yourself, "I am never going into debt."

Your parents may have incurred substantial debt that resulted in bankruptcy or the loss of their house, car, and everything they owned. The trauma of that event causes you to live in fear and save every penny you get. To you, savings equals security.

My parents owned a Mexican fast-food business that grew to seven restaurants in the Phoenix area where we lived. Growing up, I remember eating burritos and tacos for breakfast, lunch, and dinner. I loved the business and was very proud of it.

I'll never forget the day my mom and dad called my brother and I into the kitchen. As we sat around the table, Dad told us, "I have to close down the business. I can't afford to pay the bills anymore." The shock of that announcement came like a bucket of cold water thrown in my face. Panic and fear gripped me for a moment.

"We're going to have to make some changes in the way we live," Dad said. "It will take a couple of years for us to recoup our losses." This was a hard pill to swallow since our family had worked up to living in a nice house and enjoying things many of our friends did not have.

In the following weeks, we sold our home and cars and moved into a much smaller house in a working class section of town. As a high-school sophomore at the time, my self-esteem took a real beating. It was embarrassing to make the transition from relative affluence to a modest existence.

I vowed to myself, "I never want that to happen to me again!"

Although I was never angry with my parents for not making the business successful, that event shaped my life and made me a saver. Today, I need the security of having money set aside in case of a financial emergency. Now you know why I kept stalling about purchasing a dining table for our new house.

When it comes to saving, you need to ask similar questions: Why am I saving? Is it for a specific goal? Or simply to fill the need for security in my life? Compulsive squirreling away of money can be as destructive as obsessive shopping.

Saving, like spending, also has its "up" side. The ability to plan for the future and to regularly set aside money each month in a savings account requires tremendous discipline. If you or your husband or wife is a "reasonable" saver, start counting your blessings instead of your needs.

3. Using money to control your mate.

Money is often used as a way to dominate. In some marriages, whoever brings home the dough controls the purse strings.

John and Suzette had been married seven years when their third child was born. Until then, Suzette had been the money manager in the family. With three children to care for, she passed the family finance duties to her husband.

John, a middle-level manager at a national company, put in over 50 hours a week at work. After assuming the family money duties, he immediately laid out an extensive savings plan and a strict budget. "I'm giving you a monthly spending allowance," he instructed Suzette. "You can use that money to buy groceries and anything else we need. But don't ask for any more. That's it!"

Within two weeks, Suzette was out of money.

"What's wrong with you?" John demanded. "Can't you follow a simple spending plan?"

"I'm trying," his wife explained, "but there are some things you didn't take into consideration. I need money for diapers, and the kids need new shoes!"

"That's your problem!" he shouted. "You're not getting any more money!"

After six months of countless battles with John over the amount needed to take care of the family's needs, Suzette gave up. Her once cheerful smile and gracious attitude disappeared. With no extra money for make-up and clothes, even her appearance deteriorated.

To make matters worse, John spent hours lecturing his wife. "I work hard to provide for you and the kids. The least you can do is stay within our budget. You don't know how to shop because your parents spoiled you!"

Through the countless verbal assaults and his hard-nosed money management, John became the controller of his family.

This kind of behavior probably stems from underlying issues that have little to do with money. John's primary motivation may be fear of not being able to care for his family. When money and fear get mixed, however, the combination can be explosive.

Is there a positive side to a controlling money habit? Yes. But only if the controller can be convinced that he needs help to deal with the emotional problems that are driving him. A wise counselor could bring these issues into the open and help John learn to trust God to meet his needs.

4. Giving to seek approval.

Have you ever met a person who would give you the shirt off

his back if you asked him? The majority of these people are the nicest and most gracious givers on the face of the earth, but they can drive their mates mad.

Why do these people give away everything? They give to get love back. (I am not referring to biblical giving. We'll discuss that later.)

Using giving to get approval is learned at an early age. If a parent only says, "I love you," when their child draws a picture or brings home a flower, you can imagine what this teaches. The child associates receiving love with material possessions.

These love-starved children go through life, conveying the message, "Will someone please love me?" They often feel compelled to give expensive presents for every occasion — from the neighbor's birthday to Christmas gifts for everyone at work.

Not recognizing the true meaning of love can lead to obsessive giving and a frustrating marriage. The other mate views his or her spouse as an irresponsible manager of their resources — and that breeds distrust. Once the trust factor is gone, every financial decision becomes a source of contention between husband and wife.

This need to give can certainly be used in positive ways in your marriage and family. Try focusing more on doing things for others instead of giving gifts. Learn to give of yourself — but even that requires a balanced approach.

THE BALANCING ACT

Financial health begins with how well we balance our spending and saving. And balance begins with sex. No! Not *that*. I mean "gender" — male and female.

As you turn the page into the next chapter, you will discover why many arguments between a husband and wife stem from a simple fact of life: one mate is male and the other is female. God made us extremely different, but each mate was created to be the other's helper.

Learning the differences in the genders makes us more aware of how to achieve balance — especially when walking the money tightrope!

CHAPTER FOUR
MONEY & THE
GENDER PERSPECTIVE

BEFORE I got married, I thought I knew a lot about managing money. I was obviously wrong — as you already know. In fact, the older I get the more I realize how much I need to learn.

Going into marriage, I had an idealistic view of money management. I thought I would be making the big decisions like how to invest our money and which dream car to purchase. As for the daily financial details of life — like car insurance, taxes, paying doctor bills, and the rest — I figured those would be handled by Kari. After all, that's the way it had worked in my family growing up.

My mother handled all the financial details of daily living in our house. If I needed money for textbooks or my car registration was due, I usually asked Mom, and she took care of it.

Kari, however, grew up in a family where her dad took care of all the necessities of life, including car insurance, taxes, and spending money. He even returned Kari's unwanted — or ill-fitting — items back to department stores!

After two weeks of marriage the chaos caught up with us, and we began to blame one another.

Kari assumed I knew what to do. "After all," she told me, "you're the one who majored in finance at college!"

Since her dad had always taken care of the bills and making payments on time, she assumed her new husband (me!) had control of our financial situation. I complicated matters by putting up the front that I knew what I was doing when I didn't have a clue.

Kari began to panic and started calling all her friends to tell them about the mess we had gotten ourselves into.

"Why are you sharing our personal problems with everyone?" I exploded, exasperated by the embarrassment this was causing us.

"I wanted to get some help," she sobbed "I thought someone

could tell us what to do!" I could tell she was worried (husbands are so astute!), but I had no idea how to begin getting our financial affairs in order.

WHO'S JOB IS IT?

Many newly married couples return from their honeymoon with preconceived ideas about who will control the family finances.

The wife often expects her husband to assume the same money management responsibilities held by her father. This can create major problems, especially if father was Daddy Warbucks who loved spoiling his precious daughter.

When kids go to college, it is not unusual for parents to give their college kids a credit card to use for personal expenses. Dad and Mom, of course, pay off the charges and take care of the financial responsibilities for their children. This is understandable since parents want their kids to be free from worry and able to concentrate on their studies.

Imagine what happens when two college lovebirds decide to marry. Neither has learned how to budget their money because someone else (i.e., Mom or Dad) has been paying all their bills for the past 22 years. This scenario can be further complicated by different preconceived ideas concerning who should manage the household finances.

Since the groom's mom had taken care of all the finances, he naturally assumes his new wife will pay the bills, fill out forms, and call the insurance agent. The bride, on the other hand, hasn't a clue about such matters because her dad took care of her family's finances. As a result, each mate thinks it is the other's responsibility to manage household financial matters.

Friends of mine got married shortly after both graduated from college. Up to that point, Gina's dad had taken care of every detail in her life. If her car was low on gas, her dad drove it down to the gas station and filled it up. When it came time to pay for her car's registration, he handled it.

Since Dad took care of everything, she assumed Mark would do the same. Unfortunately, he had also received a lot of help from home. So each mate expected the other to assume the responsibility of money management.

"We got another bill reminder in the mail today!" Gina shouted. "How did you let that happen? It's so embarrassing!"

"Me?" Mark yelled out of frustration. "You're the wife. You're the one who should be writing the checks!"

"What do you mean?" Gina questioned. "I thought managing the money was the man's responsibility!"

Mark later confessed that he was afraid to take over control of their finances because of his lack of experience.

In a later chapter, I will share how to eliminate the control issue between couples. For now, let's concentrate on understanding the different ways men and women approach financial matters. This will help you comprehend why your mate acts a certain way.

Once you can honor your differences and begin to work as a team in this area of financial management, you will enjoy peace and security instead of frustration, worry, and fear.

MALE TRAITS AND MONEY

Let's look at five common traits regarding money management that most men share.

1. Men are expected to know how to handle money.

Most men have grown up with the assumption that they should know how to handle money wisely. Since we are expected to provide for our families (the built-in hunter's mechanism), we are also expected to know how to handle money.

An unspoken expectation exists that men are born with the ability to know how to invest, balance a checkbook, and develop spending plans. Once we are married, it is assumed that the husband will take on the responsibility of handling the couple's finances.

When Bob, a young, single pastor of a growing congregation, finally married it took time for him and his new wife to identify their strengths and weaknesses. Although Bob was a highly respected Bible teacher who could spend hours researching and planning sermons, money matters were a mystery to him. In fact, he had lived at home with his parents until he got married, and the only bill he had ever paid was his car payment.

After Bob and Sue set up housekeeping in their new apartment, it became apparent that Bob was letting bills and other important paperwork fall through the cracks. As the head of his household, however, he felt compelled to handle their finances. After all, what would people think if he didn't?

His wife, on the other hand, had been a business major in college and knew exactly how to organize their financial affairs. After years of constant conflict in this area, Sue suggested they talk with one of the church elders.

The elder went straight to the Bible and read the list of different gifts given to the body of Christ. Bob's gifts obviously lay in the areas of teaching and evangelism while Sue excelled in organization and administration.

Realizing that their differences were God-given and totally unrelated to their gender set them free to pursue their special gifting. Relieved, Bob gladly handed over the family's money matters, and Sue quickly devised a budget and set up a household accounting system.

Today, Bob proudly gives his wife all the credit for handling their financial affairs, and she respectfully submits to him as the spiritual authority in their home.

2. Men are competitive.

Like most boys, my older brother Riff and I enjoyed sports. Soccer, football, baseball, basketball, and golf were part of our everyday extracurricular activities.

"Competition" was the name of every game we played.

> GOD DOES
> WHAT WE
> CANNOT
> DO. HE
> ALTERS THE
> MAINSPRING
> AND PLANTS
> IN US A
> TOTALLY
> NEW
> DISPOSITION.
>
> OSWALD
> CHAMBERS
> (1874–1917)

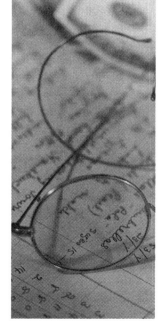

"How about a game of one-on-one?" I would challenge. *After all*, I told myself, *I'm getting pretty good at basketball.* I imagined myself bringing him to his knees and rubbing "defeated by little brother" in his face.

Riff, who is four years older, would graciously agree, "Okay, you can take the ball out first."

I would dribble to find an open

shot, stopping only long enough to get into shooting position. "Man, I'm gonna sink this one!"

Suddenly, Riff's hand would come crashing down, deflecting the ball away from the basket. Every shot I tried, Riff blocked. I couldn't even get the ball into the air.

"Ten to zip! Just like always!" he would shout. "Big brother wins again!"

"So what?" I mumbled, trying to keep him from seeing the "agony of defeat" in my teary eyes. (Thanks, Riff, for all those wonderful times!)

Defeat is a man's worst nightmare. We hate to admit it, have the word associated with us, or experience it in any way.

Unfortunately, we take that same competitive spirit with us into marriage. We are always competing against other men — from how much money we make to picking the right investment to buying a new car. Everything is done with the attitude of, "Win!" This "one-up syndrome" can wreck the family budget if a husband's spending is driven by this competitive spirit.

Dick Ebersol, president of NBC Sports, made this observation during the Atlanta Olympics: "Men will sit through the Olympics for almost anything, as long as they see some winners and losers. Women . . . want to know who the athletes are, how they got there, what sacrifices they've made. They want an attachment — a rooting interest."

When competition is missing, men will change the channel.

3. Men tend not to share weaknesses.

Men do not like to admit that they are weak in certain areas. Even if we don't have a clue about balancing a budget or investing, we will hide our inadequacies as long as possible.

When men are expected to know something, they will not admit their ignorance or their lack of knowledge.

"I thought you knew how to manage money!" the wife reprimands.

This assumption is then complicated by the husband's pride. "I do!" he retorts. "If you would stop interfering I could do a much better job."

As a man, the husband knows he is expected to be a financial whiz and will do anything to keep his wife from discovering his weakness in this area. When the evidence becomes clear, however, he defends his incompetence. The husband believes if his wife wins the argument, it will undermine his authority.

4. Men tend to be thinkers.

As men, we like to think of ourselves as being rational about decision-making. A general question that men will ask themselves is "What is the greatest reward or consequence?"

Ninety percent of all marriages have "thinker" and "feeler" types in a relationship. The thinker, usually the husband, has the ability to separate himself from the situation and look at it factually. The wife — often the "feeling" type — has trouble standing away from the situation and viewing a problem objectively.

"All our relatives are coming for Thanksgiving dinner, and the carpet in the dining room looks horrible. They'll think I'm a terrible housekeeper! We must have new carpet installed right away!" the wife exclaims, working herself into a panic attack. (I'm just making this up, of course!)

"Hold on!" the husband says as calmly as possible. "Let's think this through."

The wife takes a deep breath and finally stops wringing her hands.

"Don't forget we've been saving for our trip to the beach next summer," he reminds her. "Surely, there's an alternative to ripping up the carpet!"

"I don't know," she whines, having already decided on a new color.

"Let's call the hardware store and see how much it will cost to rent a carpet cleaning machine," he suggests. "I'll even do it myself."

A rational approach will often work — that is if the husband can keep from getting angry.

5. Men may resent the pressure of supporting the family.

Suppose a man gets up at the crack of dawn and leaves for work before anyone else in the house is awake. He puts in an exhausting and stressful 8- or 12-hour day.

When he comes home, his wife excitedly says, "We had a great day at the zoo! On the way home we stopped at the mall. How do you like my new outfit?"

After this happens a few times, the husband may resent the fact that he has to work hard to support his family while his wife is having all the fun. (I'm sure many wives feel the same way when the roles are reversed.)

My wife, Kari, stays home with our children, but she is very active. Sometimes I think she spends more time away from the house than inside. She takes the kids to the water slide, the amusement park, and other fun places.

While I know this kind of activity can also be exhausting and stressful, it still looks appealing to the guy who's trapped behind a desk day after day. When Kari tells me how much she appreciates how hard I work, however, my resentment is replaced by fulfillment.

FEMALE TRAITS AND MONEY

Women, overall, are less competitive and don't have pre-conceived ideas about what society expects from them. Their traits tend to be more on the positive side. Here are nine money traits that women share.

1. Women are cooperative.

Have you ever noticed at a church potluck dinner that women don't have to be told what needs to be done? They see an empty platter and start filling it. In the kitchen, dishes in the sink are washed and put away without anyone suggesting it be done. You will often hear, "What can I do to help?" or "I'll take care of that."

Women in general are accommodating and like to avoid conflict. Being overly cooperative, however, can result in some wives allowing themselves to become controlled by their husbands. This often leads to an unhealthy financial dependence.

Later in the book, I will share how both husband and wife can work together on a level playing field.

2. Women see the whole picture.

As opposed to the viewpoint men generally have, most women tend to make a decision based on the effect it will have on others.

Suppose Mom thinks that little Billy should have violin lessons. When she tells her husband, he says, "No, we can't afford it." End of discussion.

Everything is black and white to a man. This is why men tend to make decisions quickly. We see the facts and measure the greatest reward against the greatest consequence. Then we make a decision based on the outcome of the question.

Instead of getting angry at her husband's blunt rejection of her idea, a wife should help him understand how his decision may affect those concerned. "But, honey," Mom continues, "Billy has a real musical gift, and I think we need to foster it."

"That may be the case, but we still can't afford it," Dad declares.

Wives also need to keep in mind that husbands want to be able to say, "Yes," in most cases. When they can't, they may feel inadequate because they don't make enough money to provide for their family's every desire.

Men, on the other hand, can help women look at the facts in making decisions.

"How much will the lessons cost?" Dad asks in an effort to get a dollar amount.

"Oh! I guess I'd better find out first," Mom says, as she rushes to the phone.

When a wife realizes she needs her husband's practical approach to balance her emotional response to issues, making financial decisions becomes a team effort.

3. Women are "feelings" oriented.

Women often spend money because of the way it makes them feel. Buying an expensive dress to wear to a one-time anniversary dinner gives her a "feeling" of elegance. Having her nails done every week makes her "feel" pampered.

"Men and women don't buy for the same reasons. He simply wants the transaction to take place. She's interested in creating a relationship," writes psychologist Faith Popcorn, author of the book, *Clicking.*[1]

A friend of mine relates that he and his wife enjoy going out to dinner with another couple — let's call them Bill and Sue. Whenever Sue chooses the restaurant, she selects the most expensive place possible. Raised in a deprived environment, Sue thinks the higher the price, the better it is — no matter what quality of food is served.

Recently, the four of them ate in an upscale establishment, and my friend later told me how frustrating it was for him.

"For dessert — which alone cost $10 — they brought some type of ice cream cone, upside down," he described. "It had a lit sparkler attached and all sorts of chocolate and sugar zigzags."

My friend then gave me an itemized list of what he had figured this outrageous dessert to be worth. (Keep in mind that these figures are a pure guess!)

"Consider that a box of sparklers costs 50 cents — that's less than 4 cents for the sparkler. The ice cream is approximately 70 cents out of the grocery store freezer. Add in a few tablespoons of sugar and half a Hershey's bar, and you've got a $2 dessert for $10. Nice mark-up."

My friend can only focus on what he considers a "rip-off."

Sue, he told me, could not have been more thrilled by the gaudy dessert. At the same time, she is convinced that everyone else is also having a wonderful time!

"That's because she's not paying the check," my friend notes sarcastically. "Eighty dollars for dinner!" is how he finishes his story. That's what he remembers from the evening.

4. Women "seem" to have difficulty making decisions.

This trait relates to their being "feelings" oriented. For women, decision-making is not a cut and dried process.

A common accusation made by husbands against their wives is, "You're always changing your mind!"

That's why most stores have a "no-questions-asked" return policy. They know that women do most of the shopping, and they also know that women are indecisive. Stores realize that if women come back to return one item, they are more likely to purchase two more — which may also be returned.

Women make decisions based on a variety of conditions — most of which a man would never even think to consider.

MANY TIMES . . . THE MOST IRRITATING CHARACTERISTIC IS A BY-PRODUCT OF A QUALITY MOST RESPECTED.

JAMES C. DOBSON (1936–)

Financial decisions are often difficult for a woman because she is typically managing four or five individuals. Conversely, the husband only has to keep up with himself.

Suppose a husband comes home from work and says, "Let's get away for the weekend!"

To his surprise, the wife does not jump at the idea.

"Don't you want us to have some time to ourselves?" he asks in a wounded way.

"It's not that," she replies slowly.

Why "slowly"? Because a dozen thoughts are racing through her mind: I promised to bake cookies for Sunday school. Who will take care of the dog? Can Grandma keep the kids? None of our clothes are ironed. I need a new bathing suit — and I'd have to lose five pounds by Friday!

No wonder decision-making is difficult for a woman.

5. *Women may resent being economically dependent on their husbands.*

Although in many marriages both husband and wife work, the underlying perception is that the man should be the main breadwinner for the family. This is especially true in Christian households.

Most men are raised to assume the responsibility of providing for their family. At the same time, women — either consciously or unconsciously — accept this to be a fact of life. In most families, little girls grow up with a daddy who provides for the family.

Those wives who don't work after marriage may resent the idea of "being taken care of" by their husband. This is especially true in cases where the husband withholds money from his wife as a means of control.

Women who have had a career before marriage sometimes resent surrendering their independence — especially when it comes to money. A difficult moment for some newlyweds occurs when the new husband says to his bride, "We need to go to the bank and get a joint account." Although this is an important legal step to take, the bride may view it as an attempt to control her.

In many marriages, a couple will have "her money" and "his money." This can work as long as they have a mutual understanding. She may purchase all their clothes and make the payment on "her car." He may pay the rent, the utilities, and buy all his sports equipment.

In some cases, one or the other mate may lose out. I know one couple who has "her money" and "our money." The wife, however, jokingly goes by the adage: "What's yours is mine, and what's mine is mine!"

6. Women may resist taking on the responsibility of managing the family's money.

First of all, the wife may not like facts and figures and she may feel more comfortable doing another chore — like the gardening and yard work — to relieve her husband and give him extra time to pay the bills.

If the wife is also a working mom, she may not want the added responsibility of trying to manage the family finances. After a day at work, she is expected to fix dinner, spend time with the kids, and clean house. If, on top of these obligations, she is required to fill the role of money manager, that job will probably fall to last place on the agenda.

Being the family manager is often an overloaded task.

7. Women have a greater need for security.

Most women need to feel financially secure. This is why some women resist change.

"I'm thinking about quitting my job!" Sam states bluntly one day after work.

"What?" his wife asks, hoping he is kidding.

"I'd like to start my own business," he explains. "After all, I'm not getting any younger. I want to be my own boss."

"But how would we live?" she asks. "What about our medical insurance and your retirement fund?"

"I don't understand you!" he shouts. "Don't you want me to be successful! You never support anything I want to do!"

A husband will openly share his dreams for the future, thinking his wife will welcome the exciting news. When she reacts negatively, he withdraws.

The husband fails to realize that every time he mentions quitting this job, he yanks away his wife's security blanket.

8. Women like to consult their mates before making purchases.

Large items like cars and appliances should definitely be a combined effort between husband and wife.

Some women, however, let their husbands know they are going to be making a purchase no matter how small it may be. They don't do it to get permission, but to connect with their spouse.

"I saw the cutest little outfit for the baby the other day," she bubbles. "It's only $16, but I wanted you to see it first."

Men, on the other hand, will often neglect to include their wives when they buy something — especially if it has anything to do with tools or automobiles.

"You bought *another* lawnmower!" she screams.

Shocked by her emotional reaction, he responds, "Yeah, the one we have now isn't self-propelled."

Bill decided to buy a second car. He knew exactly what he wanted: a high-powered, emerald green sports car that had to be specially ordered from the factory. Instead of telling his wife, Marie, he decided to "surprise" her.

In the meantime, his brother-in-law called from out of state and, in passing, mentioned to Marie, "I hear Bill is getting a sports car."

"He is?" she shouted. "He didn't tell me!"

When Marie confronted her husband about his "selfish behavior," Bill meekly replied, "But I just wanted it to be a surprise."

"I'm certainly surprised!" she replied. "I'll be even more surprised when I see how you're going to fit two adults and three kids into a two-seater sports car!"

After four years of endless tension between them, Bill finally traded in his sports car for a four-door sedan. This time he made sure he consulted his wife on every detail from color to hubcaps.

9. Women give to be connected.

I don't have to tell you about all the birthday gifts and Christmas presents that wives spend hours shopping for and wrapping and sending. That's aside from Grandparents' day, Mother's day, Father's day, Valentines day, Easter — you name it, and they'll be sending a card or mailing a gift.

Most women love giving special gifts to show their appreciation. They will bake cookies for the neighbor lady who watched their kids one afternoon and make sure the church secretary has flowers for her birthday. Women are also more generous when it comes to giving to the work of God's kingdom. When a missionary family is in need, it's usually the wives who will sacrifice to give a little extra.

Kari loves to buy special gifts for her missionary friends; it's her way of making a connection and forming a bond.

She also enjoys giving gifts at Christmas. She'll make a two-page list of people she needs to buy gifts for. This list includes all her relatives, my relatives, and her past and present friends (all the way back to grade school) and anyone she has met in the past year!

I, on the other hand, have a list with only three names — Kari, Michael, and Hannah.

The gifts Kari chooses have to be exactly right. Two days before Christmas she will be at the mall, battling the holiday rush to get that perfect gift for someone.

Why is it important for women to give gifts? The exchange of gifts or the giving of something — to a ministry or charity — creates a bond that cements a friendship and provides fulfillment.

NOW YOU KNOW THE DIFFERENCE

You have probably heard of the best-selling book, *Men Are from Mars, Women Are from Venus*. The title alone suggests major differences in the way men and women think, act, and respond.

Most of our mistakes in marriage result from the distinct ways men and women are wired. How can we avoid those mistakes?

First, acknowledge the differences. Then we can move toward recognizing our gender perspectives — especially concerning money.

"What do I do with the differences?" you may be asking.

The natural reaction is to threaten, "You better change or else!" Or we try talking our mate out of their different approach to money matters: "Get with the program!"

I suggest a better method: Accept the differences with an attitude of compassion. That is the greatest single gift you can give your mate. Then go one step further and actually acknowledge any positive money traits you can identify in your mate. Be sure to focus only on the positive — not the negative traits.

For example, a wife might say to her husband, "I really appreciate the freedom you give me to buy the things we need."

He could respond, "I know you're always trying to find the best bargains. I'm glad I can trust you to spend wisely."

You may want to take a moment and list your mate's positive money traits. Then list your own attributes.

My mate's positive money habits and traits:

1.
2.
3.
4.
5.

My positive money habits and traits:
1.
2.
3.
4.
5.

Valuing each other's differences with positive affirmation is the best way to open the lines of communication.

Without communication, you will never resolve any of the money issues existing between you and your mate. In the next chapter, you will learn an exciting tool for resolving the number one conflict in marriage.

CHAPTER FIVE
RESOLVING MONEY CONFLICTS

ROBERTA, a good friend of ours, offered to help Kari out on a day that our daughter Hannah was not feeling well.

"Would you mind taking Michael to get his haircut?" Kari asked and then explained exactly how she wanted our little toddler's hair to be cut. "A little off the top and sides, but please save the curls," smiled Kari, ruffling Michael's golden locks.

With Shirley Temple curls and pudgy cheeks, Michael, at three years old, already had a real knack for charming the opposite sex — mostly those over 65. No grandma could resist patting his head and asking, "Where did you get those beautiful curls?"

As a proud dad, I always take credit for any compliments my son receives.

Since Roberta was one of Michael's favorite people, this outing was a special treat for him.

Once they arrived at the salon, Roberta repeated the instructions on cutting Michael's hair exactly as Kari had explained them to her. "A little off the sides and top — and please save the curls," Roberta said confidently.

Michael, being a big boy now, sat in his chair very quietly as the lady went to work. Roberta, feeling comfortable with her instructions, walked over to the waiting section. Several minutes passed, and Michael came running up to Roberta with a big sucker in his mouth.

"I'm all done!" he grinned.

Roberta looked up from her magazine and gasped in horror. What she saw sent shivers up her spine. Michael had been scalped — as if he had just stepped out of a military barber shop.

She stood frozen until the beautician tapped her shoulder.

"I saved the curls for his mommy," she beamed proudly, handing Roberta a baggy full of Michael's beautiful curls.

Roberta tried to think of several ways to hide the damage but knew sooner or later Kari would discover the curls were gone.

How could this have happened? she wondered miserably.

When they arrived home, Michael burst in the door. As he rounded the corner from the entryway, Roberta heard a shrill scream.

Kari was standing in the middle of the kitchen in shock.

Looking at her son she moaned, "How did this happen?"

Tearfully, Roberta explained the terrible tragedy.

When I arrived home for lunch several minutes later, I noticed Roberta leaving the house.

All she said was, "I'm so sorry."

Dashing into the house, I saw my son sitting in Kari's lap. My first thought was, *What's wrong?*

I instantly saw the problem. Our son had indeed been scalped!

In marriage, this kind of "scalping" happens more often than we like to admit. We think we have fully communicated exactly what we want to say, believing our spouse understands everything we have just shared. Time after time, however, we are left standing in shock that it did not happen the way we planned.

BUDGETING BY ATM

In most marriages, money management and planning tend to be a one-person operation. One person pays the bills, keeps the checkbook balanced, and does the investing while the other spouse enjoys the job of spending the money that was so carefully balanced.

Tension arises, however, when the managing spouse explains to the spending spouse, "There is no more money in the checking account."

"What do you mean?" the spending spouse questions defensively. "I'm not the only one who writes checks, you know!"

Or, "There must be some mistake! Maybe you subtracted wrong."

When Kari and I were first married, we were the best ATM pin number punchers in the West. Our ATM card took so much abuse that we were issued a new card just three months into our marriage.

Our "budget" was based on how far our ATM card would take us.

Near the end of the month, I would apprehensively approach the machine and hold my breath as I slid in the card, punched in the secret code, and waited. If the screen screamed, "INSUFFICIENT FUNDS" — the most hated words of the English language — I would quickly retrieve my card and hope no one behind me had noticed.

As soon as we had a zero balance, the battle began.

"Where did all the money go?" we accusingly asked one another.

"And who is going to pay the service charge on the bounced checks?"

"Where did you get your degree? From a garage sale?"

Too many couples spend their married life in conflict over money. My goal in this book is to help couples work together as a team to manage their finances.

It takes a partnership of two people learning the skills of self-control and communication to facilitate understanding. When that happens, you can work together to achieve your financial goals. Effective communication occurs when husband and wife can share openly and understand what the other is feeling — all without doing harm to the relationship.

How we choose to resolve our conflicts can lead us down a road of greater love, intimacy, and security. On the other hand, it can also lead us down the road to destruction.

WHY CONFLICTS CONTINUE

Howard Markman, Scott Stanley, and Susan Blumberg in their book, *Fighting for Your Marriage,* state that couples who have a constructive method of resolving their conflicts will almost be guaranteed a happy, fulfilling marriage.[1] Unfortunately, the majority of couples have not developed their communication skills.

If you cannot understand what your mate is trying to tell you, how will you ever resolve your conflicts? Effective communication affects every aspect of life.

My brother-in-law Randy is always eager to lend his assistance.

Once, my father called Randy and told him, "My sprinkler system has a glitch. Could you come over?"

"Sure," Randy readily offered. Working all morning, he faithfully uncovered the sprinkler system. It left ugly scars all over the yard, but hey, it had to be done, right?

Not exactly. Randy dug up the sprinklers in the back yard. Unfortunately, the problem affected the sprinklers in the *front yard!* Needless to say, some "conflict resolution" with Dad was in order.

Sometimes we need to repeat directions in order not to be misunderstood.

Even Amelia Earhart — on her first flying experience — knew the importance of proper communication: "Aren't you going to give me any dual instructions?" she asked, upon being told suddenly by an instructor that she could now take controls of the aircraft.

Often in marriage, when the financial plane is grounded — or worse, crash-landed — one partner will say to the other, "Okay, it's your turn." This abrupt "handing over of the controls" is a silent way of saying, "I can't handle it; you do it."

This type of action might temporarily relieve the one spouse, but it is quite unfair to shift all the chores onto the other. And when that happens, you guessed it, *conflict* arises.

Conflicts go unresolved for two major reasons: withdrawal and escalation.

1. Escalation of conflict.

Escalation occurs when a husband and wife raise their voices, make cutting remarks, insult one another, talk sarcastically, call each other names, demand divorce.

Couples who move into escalation will eventually rob each other of their commitment.

If the husband is quick-witted, he can hurl zingers at his wife like, "Who made you queen for a day?" Or he may snap, "What a stupid idea!" to her suggestions.

Over time, such stinging remarks will devalue the husband-wife relationship. When that happens, irreparable damage can occur.

By making hurtful comments and even going to the point of threatening divorce, couples in conflict will start questioning the commitment level of their spouse. "I don't think you love me anymore," is often the reaction of a hurting spouse.

Early in our marriage if there was any disharmony between us, Kari would instantly want to fix whatever was causing the tension. She would go on for 20 minutes, sharing her feelings and then say to me, "What do you think?"

I would respond, "I don't know."

"How can you *not* know?" she would ask, shocked by my seeming indifference.

Again I would say, "I don't know!"

"You have to know something!"

Feeling frustrated, I would sternly reply, " I DON'T KNOW!"

Kari would whine, "You must not care about me or our family."

Oftentimes men, like myself, just don't know. We are thrown into conversations that turn into full-scale battles, and we don't even know how they started.

After Kari and I would get to the point of my saying "I don't know," the conflict moved from escalation to withdrawal.

2. Withdrawal from conflict.

I always considered myself a lousy debater. Whenever Kari and I got into a conflict, I would usually walk away from the conversation.

Little did I know, I was acting like 85 percent of all men. When it comes to arguing or debating, men are less proficient in verbal skills than women. I know a few men who can compete verbally with a woman, but most of them clam up and refuse to communicate during a conflict.

Why do men choose to withdraw? From the time we are young, boys learn rules for everything we do. Take little league baseball, for instance. When I played little league, I quickly realized that the coach was not there to let us have fun (although that is why I signed up!).

I vividly remember my first day of baseball practice. I sat on the bench the entire time. The coach went over all the rules of the game from the proper mechanics of hitting and throwing to catching a baseball.

In general, men go through life sitting on a bench listening to rules. Then we go out and perform according to how we were instructed. Everything men do is coordinated around a rule book. Work, sports, how we drive a car, run a business, take care of our children — even how we fight our wars with other countries.

The only area where we don't have any

MONEY AND

MARRIAGE . . .

ARE THE TWO

THINGS THAT

MAKE MEN AND

WOMEN DEVILS

OR SAINTS.

OSWALD CHAMBERS

(1874–1917)

type of agreement or rule book is marriage. So when we get in that "Uh oh, what do I do now?" phase, we walk away. (Keep in mind that some women are also part of this withdrawal group.)

In addition, a man feels that the home is his castle, and he should feel safe from any verbal conflict. After a hard day at the office, job site, or even a long day on the golf course, the last thing on a husband's mind is talking when he gets home. On the other hand, the wife is excitedly waiting for him to walk in to door so she can talk.

Picture the husband for a moment. He blasts through the door ready to get his hands on the daily newspaper. On the way to the Lazy-boy, his wife intercepts and starts forcing him to think.

"It's family night, you know," she states, well aware that the thought had never entered his mind. "Do you have anything planned?"

"I don't know," he responds. "How about we go get pizza?"

She shoots back, "We did that last week."

Instead of looking up from the paper and giving his eyes and ears to his beautiful wife, he grunts, "How about we discuss this later?"

Instantly she snaps, "That's what you said yesterday."

Inside, the man says to himself, *She nags too much and talks too much. When will she start leaving me alone?*

And the wife stands there thinking, *Why doesn't he ever talk or listen to me? He will never understand — or maybe he doesn't care about me and the kids.*

Since she feels disconnected, the wife tries harder to get a meaningful response. Then she will start talking about their relationship, the kids' relationships, in-law relationships, and the list goes on. In the mean time, the gap between the wife and her husband widens.

When this happens, most women fail to realize that men are not pulling away from intimacy and relationship, but rather we are pulling away from the potential conflict.

HOW TO "PLAY BALL"

What subject creates the most conflicts in marriage? You guessed it — money! When the wallet is involved, we instantly go on the alert. Our future, security, and stomachs involve money — all the more reason why we need to be in unison with our spouse regarding what we do with our money.

How can we develop an effective way to resolve our conflicts that will eliminate frustrations and hurt feelings on both sides?

RESOLVING MONEY CONFLICTS

Kari and I learned a method that not only resolved our conflicts, but ultimately eliminated any frustrations and hurt feelings. We call it "Play Ball."

This method has been taught by many experts, including Stephen Covey. Drs. Howard Markman and Scott Stanley have researched this technique for 15 years and have found it to be an important ingredient to making love in marriage last forever.

Most conflicts result from failing to be heard. One spouse will walk out of the discussion, or the conflict will escalate into a shouting match in which neither can be heard or understood. "Play Ball" is used whenever a conflict escalates to a war.

When Kari and I employ the "Play Ball" method we use a small cushion ball as the object of discussion. Whoever has the ball in their possession is the "talker," and the one not holding the ball is the "listener." Let's look at the rules to this successful game where both teams win:

1. The speaker is the person who is in possession of the ball.

2. The listener is the person who is *not* in possession of the ball.

3. The speaker speaks in small segments on their feelings without accusation. (Speaker is not permitted to use "you" in a statement that points to the listener as guilty.)

4. The speaker must use the "I" method speaking. ("I" don't like to be put into a situation that. . . .)

5. After the speaker is finished with their small statement, he/she then passes the ball to the listener.

6. The listener is now the speaker (in possession of the ball) and repeats back what the speaker said when he or she had the ball. (This repetition is why the speaker must talk in small segments. It also forces the listener to listen carefully.)

7. When the speaker "feels" the listener has fully heard and understands everything he/she has shared, the ball is passed and the roles reversed until both sides have been able to share and be heard.

8. After both sides feel heard and understood, you stop and set a time and date to come back together and discuss resolutions.

9. It is crucial to understand one another fully before finding a solution to the conflict.

The solution stage comes later — after you have both had time to digest the information shared by your partner.

TALKERS AND THINKERS

In many marriages, communication often comes to a sudden stop when both husband and wife have finally come to understand each other. Why? Because one spouse has the gift of saying what he or she is thinking before actually thinking about what he or she is saying.

Kari has that gift. Let me give you an example of how this phenomenon works.

Kari and I planned a special vacation to a marriage conference to relax and hear some great speakers. On the way to the airport, we got into a discussion.

After sharing our thoughts, she started trying to resolve the issue. While she was explaining her ideas to me, I turned her off and began criticizing her suggestions. The more she shared, the more upset I became.

Why? Kari was demanding that I share with her my thoughts and ideas on the discussion. But how could I do that? I didn't even know what I felt about the issue. If I had been honest and told her, "I have no opinion," I knew she would respond with, "You don't care!"

I just needed time to think about what she was sharing, and I wasn't given that opportunity. (Usually one mate will need time to think out the situation before trying to come to a resolution.)

Needless to say, that incident put a damper on the first days of our vacation.

You and your mate most likely have different ways of communicating your thoughts and ideas. It can be very helpful to identify your particular communication personality.

One such test, the Taylor-Johnson, helps couples pinpoint certain key elements to their personalities. At the marriage conference, we took part in this particular evaluation and learned valuable information about each other.

First, I realized that my brain is often so busy trying to comprehend what Kari is saying that I am unable to speak. I need time to assimilate all of the input she is feeding me.

In other words, I have to think before I can talk. After I have time to process all the incoming information, I am then able to come up with helpful solutions for the problem-solving process.

Kari, on the other hand, needs to talk to think. By identifying our unique communication personalities, Kari and I finally realized why we had problems communicating.

During the marriage conference, friends of ours, Chuck and Barb Snyder, shared how they resolve conflicts. Kari and I found that we were similar to the Snyders in our communication methods.

Chuck's wife, Barb, loves to talk to think and immediately shares what is on her mind. Meanwhile, Chuck needs time to take it all in, just like me. They shared with us several humorous incidents they had encountered before they understood one another's unique communication personality.

After spending a late night with our friends talking and laughing, Chuck and Barb shared how they learned to stop arguments before they grew into battles. "The most important step is to stop talking as soon as both parties have had a chance to share their feelings," they told us.

The information we brought home from our trip changed the way we communicated with each other. Kari and I gained a greater understanding of why we react in certain ways.

HEARING AND UNDERSTANDING

What is the number one desire in communication? To be heard. When we hear and understand each other, we are on the way to successfully resolving our conflicts.

After both sides have been heard, the process of finding a solution comes next. Solutions come only after both partners have been heard — as in "Play Ball."

The next process can possibly be the most important step in resolving conflicts. It can also be the easiest since both partners have already had the opportunity to present their feelings.

Feelings can *never* be wrong. They must be heard and understood. "Play Ball" can help make that possible.

Like most men, Chuck and I need to step back and get away from the situation to think about what has been said.

If Kari confronts me with an issue that is bothering her — and then gives me the opportunity to "mull it over" (sometimes up to three days) — I can better resolve our problem.

My finest ideas and understanding never come when I am face to face with Kari. Rather, my best solutions occur while I am mowing the yard, running eight miles, or driving to the office.

After I have had the opportunity to think through the situation, then Kari and I can come back to our conversation and offer solutions. This is why a set meeting time is crucial. Both partners need to commit to a specific time to talk and then be faithful to honor that commitment.

Since I have had time to think about what happened between us, I can now reasonably begin the process of conflict solution. I no longer feel threatened by Kari. Oftentimes I will start the solution phase by asking Kari, "How could I have behaved better?" or "What would you like to see happen?"

Sounds simple and easy, doesn't it? And it really is if you follow the simple steps of Play Ball.

After our talk with Chuck and Barb, Kari told me, "I no longer see you as a husband who doesn't care about me and who has nothing to offer to a problem-solving conversation."

(I must have been a real bimbo!)

"Rather," she told me, "I understand your unique communication personality. Now I see you as an individual who needs to take time to think things through."

Wives, maybe your husband is like me — a thinker, not a talker. Maybe the guy just needs time to stop and ponder what you are telling him.

Husbands, you need to make the commitment to follow through and Play Ball by finding a solution to the problem at hand.

Your husband or wife has one main desire for your relationship: to be heard and understood.

> HAVE YOUR HEART RIGHT WITH CHRIST, AND HE WILL VISIT YOU OFTEN, AND SO TURN WEEKDAYS INTO SUNDAYS, MEALS INTO SACRAMENTS, HOMES INTO TEMPLES, AND EARTH INTO HEAVEN.
>
> CHARLES H. SPURGEON (1834–1892)

GREEN LIGHT THINKING

After husband and wife have had time to Play Ball and come up with ideas for solutions, you can come together for round two.

Problem solving can actually be the easiest part of this procedure. In fact, it can become a vehicle that leads to greater intimacy.

Both parties have shared ideas, solutions, and anything that is related to bringing the conflict to a close. The key is sharing without being criticized. A critical spirit — from either spouse — can destroy the entire system immediately.

"Green Light Thinking" finishes the solution process. Let me outline this phase:

1. Brainstorm.

Begin by sharing numerous ideas (the more the better) that can bring about a win-win situation for both husband and wife. Once all the ideas have been written down for both mates to see, the procedure to find a win-win solution begins.

2. Eliminate.

Go through the list and cross out any ideas that either spouse may dislike. If only one spouse dislikes an idea, it can be crossed out. Circle the ones that appeal to both husband and wife. Before you can circle an idea, however, both must agree that it is acceptable.

3. Discuss.

Once the list has been dissected, each spouse can discuss why a particular idea will bring a win-win for both. At this point the discussion turns into one of enjoyment.

4. Agree.

When you agree on a solution that makes both husband and wife equally happy, you feel safe because no one gets the short end of the deal.

Many battles intensify because one spouse feels that he/she will be losing something. With green light thinking, the ability to share ideas and feelings — without the fear of being shamed — will bring calmness, gentleness, and greater understanding.

THE BATTLE OF THE ATM

A married couple we know had been in the middle of a major conflict for several months. Gary had always been an ATM machine away from a good time. Each month he would stay within the budget and felt he was doing his job by not overspending.

Meanwhile, his wife, Christy, would balance the checkbook at the end of the month and find her numbers off. As a perfectionist, Christy was frustrated because her checkbook was never balanced correctly. In an effort to discover the mistakes, she confronted her husband.

"The checkbook won't balance. Are you taking money out of the ATM without telling me?" she questioned.

"I guess I did forget to give you a few ATM receipts," he admitted.

At that point the battle of the ATM began.

Each day as soon as Gary arrived home, Christy would be like a patriot missile, locking in on her target, ready to destroy. "Did you take any money out of the ATM today?" she fired off.

"Get off my back, would you?" Gary shot back. Like 85 percent of withdrawers, he then retreated into the bunker (the Lazy-boy — with remote in hand).

After many confrontations, Christy was frustrated, and Gary felt unjustly accused.

Having recently learned the Play Ball method, they decided to give it a try to help resolve the ATM conflict.

Since he was holding the ball first, Gary started the game.

"I feel my forgetting to give you the ATM receipts shouldn't be such a big deal that it causes an argument," he shared as calmly as possible. "As long as we can figure it out at the end of the month, what difference does it make?"

"So what you're saying is," Christy repeats back, "that you feel it's not a big deal if you forget the receipts."

"No, I'm saying that my forgetting to show you the receipts shouldn't lead to an argument that hurts my feelings or makes me feel like I'm being yelled at," Gary replied.

"So you're saying, you feel very hurt when I get upset at you for forgetting the receipts," Christy echoed.

"YES, that's what I feel!!!" shouted Gary.

He then tossed the ball gently to Christy who then shared her feelings.

"You always go to the ATM's . . ." started Christy but then caught herself making a "you" accusation. Remembering this was an opportunity to share her feelings she backtracked and began with, "Whenever I sit down and try to balance the checkbook, and the bank statement does not match, I feel I have failed."

"I hear you saying that when you don't match the checkbook register with the bank's statement, you feel you have failed," Gary responded.

"Yes, if I have the tools necessary to balance the checkbook, I can do it. But if I don't, I get frustrated because I feel that I have failed," replied Christy.

"Because you don't have the ATM receipts to balance the checkbook with the bank's statement, you get frustrated," repeated Gary.

"Exactly," responded Christy.

After talking and repeating several more times, Gary and Christy quit the Play Ball process because each felt that the other truly heard and understood what was being shared.

"Tomorrow at lunch time, let's use Green Light ideas to resolve the problem," Gary suggested.

The entire Play Ball process only took them 10 minutes. Gary was now able to understand Christy's feelings and why she would ambush him at the end of every month.

After their talk, Gary went to play basketball at the park, and Christy walked over to a friend's house.

On his drive home, Gary thought about all the different ways he could make sure he gave his wife the ATM receipts. He felt responsible for keeping the checkbook balanced and was thrilled she worked so hard on their finances.

Meanwhile, Christy shared with her friend. "I've been so hard on Gary. I know we're still adjusting to married life, and he has been doing such a great job spending time with me and making me feel important as his wife."

The next day at lunch Gary and Christy had a constructive conversation about their problem.

Gary immediately provided a solution. "I will give you the receipts of all ATM transactions the same day I make them."

"I'm sorry for being so insensitive," Christy responded. "I will not take it personally when I don't have all the ATM receipts to balance the checkbook."

Using Green Light thinking took them a mere five minutes to discuss and resolve.

Resolving conflicts doesn't require a degree in counseling or attendance at every marriage seminar within driving distance. All you and your mate need is the desire to change, a willingness to learn new methods of conflict resolution, and the determination to move your marriage from the battleground to the amusement park.

It may take time, but, with God's help, you can begin to resolve conflicts before they even begin.

DATE NIGHT OR DATE FIGHT?

It is Friday night, and Thomas comes home from work ready for "date night" with his wife. They arrive at their favorite seafood restaurant and begin sharing their day with each other.

During the appetizers, he mentions to her that he has to leave town Monday to meet with a business client.

Surprised, his wife responds sharply, "You never told me about leaving on Monday. Why didn't you mark the date in my calendar?"

Feeling wrongly accused, Thomas replies, "I told you about it months ago. It was your responsibility to write in *your* calendar book."

"I have never heard you mention this business trip! You always do this to me. I hate hearing at the last minute that you're going out of town," lashes back his wife. "Your job is more important to you than your family."

Feeling wrongly accused, Thomas whispers harshly, "You just don't appreciate all that I do."

Needless to say the rest of the date is ruined.

I'm sure we have all experienced these date fights on date night.

Are you so busy that you and your mate do not take time to be alone together without kids or friends? When you finally make time for a date, a battle erupts, and you end up rushing through your candle-light dinner to retreat home for cover.

"What a night!" is often said at the end of a time that was supposed to be intimate and refreshing. Instead, you are more exhausted and discouraged than before the date started.

What can you do to eliminate the tension during the few quality times you get together?

MAKING MARRIAGE F.U.N.

Kari and I discovered a concept that has brought back sponta-neous fun and intimacy to our relationship — like when we were first dating. Many couples I know struggle with this simple yet very difficult activity because they simply forget how to do it.

This simple concept, called "Having F.U.N.," can take your marriage to a new level. When you are having a special F.U.N. date or activity, you must stick to the F.U.N. rules.

1. Fulfilling.

If you forget to add this ingredient to your recipe for a fulfilling marriage, it can come out tasting bitter.

When was the last time you went on a date or had an hour at home together without any distractions — and just had fun? How long has it been since you and your spouse spent time laughing, playing, or just dreaming about the future?

2. Under no circumstances.

Under no circumstances is any serious matter to be brought up. Any conversation that is not fun to talk about is kept safely locked up until a designated time.

Kari and I have gained great confidence in one another knowing that, when we designate "fun" time, nothing can be discussed that has the potential to cause conflict. We don't have to "walk on eggshells," but can be free to be ourselves.

3. Never.

Never take advantage of having your spouse alone to bring up serious conflicts in your marriage. Unless your time alone was designated as a problem-solving time, leave the problem at home. Otherwise, your spouse will feel defensive and "set up."

Drs. Howard Markman and Scott Stanley suggest that both spouses simply state to each other that the time they are spending together is just for "fun." Then couples can be more open with one another and enjoy true intimacy.

If you and your mate decide to keep the F.U.N. rules, your spare time won't become a business meeting about money, relatives, friends, budget, or whatever else creates an opportunity for conflict.

Kari and I started keeping the F.U.N. rules on our date nights four years ago and experienced drastic improvements just after one evening. At first it was difficult to remind each other, but the results were extremely positive. Now our date nights are more fun than when we were dating before marriage!

FROM PLUMS TO COCONUTS

When Kari and I moved to Missouri, we were expecting our first child, Michael. Our friends, who already lived in Branson, allowed us to move into an apartment above their garage. The place was very nice with two bedrooms, a bathroom, and a living room, but it had no real kitchen at the time. As a result, I ate cereal and poptarts for breakfast before leaving for work each morning.

One day after returning home from work, Kari greeted me at the door and with a big smile said, "Guess who's coming to visit us?"

Excited, I blurted out my guess. "Is it my parents?"

Kari smiled and said, "Yes! They're going to rent a cabin nearby."

Instantly, I blurted out, "Finally, I can have a big home-cooked breakfast again!"

Kari's big smile turned to an instant frown. I knew I was in trouble. I had no intentions of making Kari feel bad, but I was honestly looking forward to having a good, home-cooked breakfast.

During this time I was into exercising and working out with weights. This regimen — especially lifting weights — kept me hungry 24 hours a day. For the weightlifter, breakfast is the biggest and most important meal of the day. Since we did not have access to a kitchen, I ate 14 bowls of cereal and a half dozen pop tarts before I felt somewhat full.

When I heard my mom was coming, I was excited because I knew her cabin included a fully-equipped kitchen. All I could think about was bacon and eggs, hash browns and biscuits!

Kari, at the time, was seven months pregnant with our first child, and breakfast was not exactly her favorite meal of the day. Her energy level was low, and the summer heat was also taking its toll.

Getting up in the morning to fix a "big breakfast" — even in the microwave — was far from appealing to Kari. Living in an apartment without a kitchen made it next to impossible anyway. I knew that and had never complained.

Later that day, Kari let me know how my remark had affected her. Without knowing it, she used a powerful word picture that taught us a valuable lesson in communication.

In their book, *The Language of Love,* noted authors Dr. Gary Smalley and Dr. John Trent explain the importance of word pictures in our daily lives.[2]

Some of the greatest leaders of all time — Winston Churchill, Abraham Lincoln, Benjamin Franklin, and Ronald Reagan — all used word pictures to communicate their messages. Other world leaders have used word pictures to manipulate and bring a nation together for evil.

Walt Disney was a master at communicating through word pic-

tures. With one movie, the sport of deer hunting took a heavy blow. Watching Bambi running through the woods, making friends, having fun, and being dependent upon his mother captured the hearts of children, moms, and even the tough, no-emotion, gun-toting dads.

When audiences heard the gun shot that killed Bambi's mother, they no longer saw deer as a prey to provide meat for dinner, but as an important family member. Walt Disney, through the power of an animated word picture, touched the hearts of countless hunters who saw their target as Bambi's mom.

The word picture Kari used immediately put me in touch with her feelings. Like a movie, I could see how my comment had affected her.

"Roger, can I share something with you?" Kari asked when I came home from work that evening. "Today you made the comment about finally getting a home-cooked meal, and that really hurt my feelings. I felt as if you had thrown a coconut at my head. It was hard and swift and knocked me to the ground."

"My comment about a home-cooked meal felt like a coconut being thrown at your head?" I asked, shocked that my remark had such a negative impact. "Wow, that really must have hurt."

"It did hurt," she said. "I know you did not mean to hurt me, but I just wanted you to know how I felt."

She continued. "Right now I am seven months pregnant, and I don't have a kitchen to cook in or to prepare food for you. I would love to get up and cook you breakfast if I could, but without a kitchen I can't do it. Besides, I warned you before we got married that I don't *do* breakfast. Your comment this morning had an impact on me as a wife. Even though it may have appeared like a raisin or grape to you, it felt like a coconut to me."

I got the picture.

Realizing my insensitivity, I instantly took her in my arms and asked forgiveness.

Since that day, Kari and I measure any undesirable comments based on the size or weight of fruit. It may be corny, but it works for us. Her word picture became a secret code for conveying our feelings.

If she says to me, "You just hit me with a plum," I know I hurt her, but I can measure the degree of negative impact with the size of fruit she describes. If she calls my comment an orange, cantaloupe, or a watermelon, I know exactly the amount of harm I have done.

One day she told me, "You just dropped a watermelon on my head!" Immediately, I pictured myself standing on top of a tall building dropping this large piece of fruit on my wife's head.

With her "fruity" word picture, Kari created a tool that has helped our family communicate hurt feelings in a non-threatening way. If we make comments that offend each other or our kids, we can instantly brand it with a fruit.

THREE BENEFITS OF WORD PICTURES

The greatest Communicator in history used word pictures to convey difficult spiritual truths to His disciples.

In the beginning of Christ's ministry, a large group of people congregated to hear what He had to say. When Jesus saw a boat sitting on the shore, He went over and sat in it so all the people could see and hear Him. Instead of giving them hard facts, Jesus shared word pictures.

"A farmer was sowing grain in his fields. As he scattered the seed across the ground, some fell beside a path, and the birds came and ate it. And some fell on rocky soil where there was little depth of earth; the plants sprang up quickly enough in the shallow soil, but the hot sun soon scorched them and they withered and died, for they had so little root. Other seeds fell among thorns, and the thorns choked out the tender blades. But some fell on good soil, and produced a crop that was thirty, sixty, and even a hundred times as much as he had planted" (Matt. 13:3-8).

Then Jesus said, "If you have ears, listen!"

Let's see what we can learn from Jesus about being an effective communicator.

1. Word pictures bring communication to life.

Farming was a way of life for people in the time of Christ, and He often used familiar images related to agriculture to get His point across.

Until Kari and I got married and moved to the Ozarks — the farming Promised Land — I was anything but a country boy. In fact, I had grown up in the valley of Los Angeles, where land was at a premium and a small property lot cost hundreds of thousands of dollars. Needless to say, no one was planting crops or raising cattle on the manicured lawns of Southern California. As a result, farming was a mystery to me.

When we first moved to Missouri and built our house in the country, we were excited about country living. Almost immediately, we decided it would be nice to have some turkeys.

One day Kari and I and the kids drove out to a local turkey farm.

"We'd like to buy a turkey," I told the farmer who led us to a large fenced area where dozens of the big birds were scratching in the dirt.

"There's a good one," the farmer told me, pointing out the good turkeys from the bad ones. I had never even visited a real farm before much less seen a live turkey, so they all looked the same to me.

"Go ahead and pick him up," the farmer instructed, knowing he was in for a good laugh.

I didn't even think twice about it. With a big smile on my face, I walked right into the area where all the turkeys were pecking and cackling.

"There's a nice one," Kari said.

As soon as I reached down to pick up the turkey, the bird suddenly turned on me. I felt as if I had just entered the ring with Mike Tyson. Panic swept over me. I was hit with a left wing then a right wing followed by an upper cut to the jaw.

With my head spinning, I looked over at the farmer and my wife, who were doubled over with laughter. It was apparent I hadn't "gone the distance" with this turkey.

"Here, let me show you the way to do it," the farmer suggested somewhat sympathetically. "The trick is to pick him up and turn him upside down. Then he can't flap his wings."

Thanks a lot! *Why didn't he tell me that in the beginning?* I wondered.

If the farmer had told me, "Body slam the turkey and grab its claws," I would have known exactly how to handle him.

As wannabe farmers, our family now raises cows, a horse, ducks, chickens, guineas, geese, an emu, a pig, and a pot belly pig named Wilma! Today, farming word pictures have greater meaning to me.

Like the individuals sitting on the lakeshore listening to Christ, they could picture in their minds the image Christ was portraying because they had often seen farmers sowing seed — and had probably done so themselves. That is why Jesus said, in the beginning and the end of His parable, to "listen." It was so simple, yet he knew some would not understand the analogy He was making.

2. Grab and direct attention.

In marketing, this method used to grab and direct our attention is called "branding." Many commercials and advertisements aim at branding their products.

When you think of shipping a letter or a gift, and it needs to be there overnight, what delivery service come to mind? FedEx, of course. Federal Express has taken overnight delivery and branded it into our minds with "when it absolutely, positively has to be there overnight."

At my office, when we put together a project that needs to be classy, we say, "Make it 'Polo' quality." Since Ralph Lauren is known for having classy, professional clothing, that's the look we strive to achieve in our business presentation.

"Branding" grabs your attention and has direct meaning.

When Kari shares a "fruit" analogy with me, I instantly know what she means. If she tells me that I have dropped a watermelon on her head from eight stories high, I quickly realize how much my words have hurt our relationship.

3. Word pictures lock into our memory.

Advertisers spend millions of dollars a year to develop concepts to make us remember to buy their products.

Every time you need a flashlight battery, what comes to mind? The Energizer Bunny, of course. How many times have we used their slogan, "Nothing outlasts the Energizer"?

Through emotional word pictures, you and your spouse can have your own built-in, tailor-made communication method that ultimately brings instant understanding, sympathy, and forgiveness.

The best part is, you'll have a captive audience — your spouse.

CRASH-PROOF PROTECTION

Even in the best of marriages, conflict can accelerate like a teenager in a drag race. You can avoid a collision and enjoy a smooth, safe ride, however, by applying the simple, yet effective conflict-resolving tips outlined in this chapter. (How's that for a word picture?)

The Play Ball method and word pictures are the best "crash-proof protection" communication methods for marriages — or any relationship. To facilitate any effective communication method, however, takes discipline and understanding.

In some cases, I encourage couples to seek out the help of a professional counselor who can keep both husband and wife accountable to using the prescribed method of communication — whether it's Play Ball, word pictures, or some other positive technique. Communication is the only way to resolve conflict and the ticket to building a marriage that will last a lifetime.

Now that the highway of communication has been opened between you and your mate, you can get down to where "the rubber meets the road." In the next chapter, you will learn how to drive the frustration, worry, and fear created by money problems right out of your marriage.

CHAPTER SIX
RUNNING THE FAMILY BUSINESS

WHEN a top executive with General Electric initiated divorce proceedings to end his marriage of over 30 years, the story made national headlines.

Although his wife had never worked outside the home, she felt entitled to half of their estate. The husband, on the other hand, refused to meet her demands, saying he was the one who had earned the money.

Why did this divorce capture the interest of the American people? Because a housewife was battling for what was rightfully hers. She worked to help put him through school, took care of his children while he put in many hours at the office, and managed all the household affairs. The husband, of course, had worked hard to provide for his family so they could live a comfortable life.

This battle goes beyond the money issue to one of respect and appreciation. How could a couple who has spent many years together and has grown children allow their marriage to deteriorate to this point? What could have kept this from happening?

Many married couples end up spiritually, emotionally, and mentally bankrupt because they fail to see the dynamics at work in the marriage relationship. Marriage and family life — like any other endeavor — require planning, hard work, and commitment — the kind of effort you would put into running your own business. Maybe that's how we need to view marriage — like a family business.

With that analogy in mind, let's consider what it would take to run a successful family business.

SEEING THE BIG PICTURE

Jack Stack, a manager/supervisor for a national machine company, was given the opportunity — along with some other managers and supervisors — to buy the business when it went bankrupt. Seeing no other alternative, this group decided purchasing the company was the best way to keep their jobs.

In 1983, Stack took over control of a company that had no money, zero outside resources, and employed 119 people who needed salaries to pay mortgages and put food on the table and clothes on their backs. He knew the survival of the company depended upon each and every individual who worked there.

Springfield Remanufacturing Corporation turns old engines into engines that work like new. The labor is not glamorized. In fact, most of the people leave work covered in grease and dirt. What did Stack do to turn the company around from losing over $60 thousand a year to annual sales of more than $70 million? He got the employees involved.

NOT WHERE I BREATHE, BUT WHERE I LOVE, I LIVE.

ROBERT SOUTHWELL (1561–1595)

By presenting them with the big picture, each employee knew exactly the impact his job had on helping make the company a success. From the top executives to the cleanup crew, every person knew how he or she fit into the big picture. Like pieces to a puzzle scattered on a tabletop, Springfield Remanufacturing initially seemed disjointed. But once the pieces started coming together from the edges, and were worked toward the middle, the company became a cohesive and impressive picture.

How would employees be able to save money if they didn't know where expenses needed to be cut? Stack knew that to make the company profitable, everyone needed to see the complete financial picture. Stack instituted a weekly meeting at which employees came together to review the company's income statement.

As a result, employees were motivated to eliminate waste and work more efficiently. By including and educating people on why they did a particular job and its impact on the company, Stack created a family of employees who felt they were contributing not only to the business but to their own success. That attitude made Springfield Remanufacturing a thriving business.

By following the procedures used by Jack Stack, your marriage can reach the same level of success. First, however, you need to ask yourself several questions:

- What is your "big picture"?
- Do you have a family mission, value, or purpose statement?
- Are your kids and your spouse involved in decision-making?
- Are you having a weekly meeting to talk about the family business?

Dear friends of ours shared how they meet every morning for a devotional time together. Then they review their plans for the day and address any issues of concern.

"Maybe we should try that," I told Kari.

"Sounds good to me," she agreed, "especially since our days are usually packed out with little time left for ourselves."

As an early bird, I was accustomed to waking up and having my devotions before I went to work. Kari, on the other hand, liked to take advantage of a full morning's sleep.

Now we both wake up at six o'clock and have our devotional and prayer time. Then we go over our schedule for the day and discuss any other family plans or projects.

I didn't know it at the time, but Kari and I were mirroring the kind of meeting that a Fortune 500 company convenes. Communication, strategic planning, brainstorming sessions, and finances were all being covered the way the big guys do it.

What did this do for us? It *increased* our communication and *decreased* our conflicts. Sounds like a win-win situation to me!

The apostle Paul, in writing to believers at Philippi, challenged them with this statement: "Then make me truly happy by loving each other and agreeing wholeheartedly with each, working together with one heart and mind and purpose" (Phil. 2:2).

A husband and wife are a team, where each member makes a 50/50 contribution — not 75/25 or 60/40 or 90/10. In marriage, there are no stars, ball hogs, or benchwarmers. Marriage is "working together with one heart and mind and purpose."

Now that we recognize the importance of unity, how do we

achieve it? Let's look at several steps you can take to attain unity in your marriage:

- Leave and cleave.
- Stick to your job description.
- Create a "value statement."
- Develop a family business handbook.

LEAVING AND CLEAVING

The day Kari and I got married, I walked my mom down the church aisle to her seat before the ceremony. When I sat her down and turned around to start walking away, tears rolled down my cheeks.

These were not tears of joy at being free from my parents' control, but of sadness. I knew my life would never be the same.

That sense of security, knowing Mom and Dad had always been there for me, would be gone. From the time I graduated from pre-school to my college graduation, my parents had always been there for me. In fact, I don't think they missed a single event in my life.

I understand why God's says, "Leave!" He knows that as children we become dependent upon our mother and father — not only to provide food and clothes — but also to provide emotional support during the hard times and to shout joyfully with us during the good times.

"For this reason a man will leave his father and mother and be united to his wife, and the two shall become one flesh" (Eph. 5:31;NIV).

If we fail to establish a support-based relationship with our mate — from the very beginning of the marriage — we will never experience the unity of being one. The lives of husband and wife are so intimately intertwined that what happens to one automatically affects the other. No matter how hard you try, your behavior — and the consequences of that behavior (good or bad) — have an impact on your mate.

By establishing "a leaving and cleaving relationship" those dependent ties with your parents are cut off, and you are brought into a deeper relationship with your mate — and with God. With all the problems that can occur in marriage, leaving and cleaving makes it harder to run back to Mom and Dad. Instead, you are now running to your Father in heaven for guidance. By having to go to God for help, you will become more dependent upon Him.

RUNNING THE FAMILY BUSINESS
THE HUSBAND'S JOB DESCRIPTION

You are probably familiar with the scriptural mandate of leadership given to husbands: "For the husband is the head of the wife as Christ is the head of the church. . . . Husbands, love your wives, just as Christ loved the church, and gave himself up for her" (Eph. 5:23-25;NIV).

According to this passage, what are the husband's responsibilities in the marriage relationship? Let's look at three specific mandates.

1. The husband provides leadership.

The Message Bible translation puts it this way: "The husband provides leadership . . . not by domineering but by cherishing." Scripture clearly states that the husband is to be a leader. How? By "cherishing," not "domineering."

The definition of leadership has changed dramatically in the last 50 years. Until recently, a leader was viewed as the ultimate authority. In the 1990s, leadership has been redefined and taken to a new level in the business world. Actually, it has not been redefined, but has been given a new paradigm to be like what Christ had in mind for husbands.

Author Stephen Covey defines leaders as "pathfinders" who are out front making sure the business is headed in the right direction. What direction might that be? In a direction that will keep their organization healthy.

Husbands have a similar responsibility. They must keep the family going in a direction that is healthy.

2. The husband loves his wife.

As part of their leadership role, the husband is told to love his mate. "Husbands, love your wives, just as Christ loved the church, and gave himself up for her" (Eph. 5:25;NIV).

Men apparently need more instruction than women when it comes to "love." How is a man to love his wife? Unconditionally — with no strings attached. To help husbands grasp this concept, the apostle Paul provides a word picture. Men are to love their wives "as Christ loved the church."

What image comes to mind? Christ dying for us on the cross so we could have everlasting life (John 3:16). You don't get anymore unconditional than that.

In his book, *1001 Great Stories and Quotes,* author R. Kent Hughes, provides this story:

Cyrus the Mede, the great conqueror of Babylon and the then-known world, had a general under his authority whose wife was accused of treason. The woman was tried before a tribunal, found guilty, and sentenced to death. After the sentence was announced, the general went to Cyrus with this request: "King Cyrus, please let me take her place."

Cyrus, in awe at what the general asked, said to his court, "Can we terminate a love as great as this?" Cyrus relaxed the sentence and paroled the woman to her husband. As the two left the court, the general said to his wife, "Did you see the benevolent look in Cyrus' eyes as he pardoned you?" The wife responded, "I only had eyes for the one who loved me enough that he was willing to die for me."[1]

That's the kind of love God expects from a husband.

3. *The husband serves his family.*

The greatest leader is one who gives. He does not take. We have only to look at Jesus. "The Son of Man did not come to be served, but to serve" (Matt. 20:28;NIV).

In sports, the true leaders on any team are usually not the highest scorers or the best paid. Instead, it's often the guys whose names hardly show up on the stat sheets.

For example, in basketball, it is the point guard's duty to get the basketball into the hands of the shooters who are in scoring position. This is the position I played in high school and college. For me to be effective for the team, I often had to sacrifice my own opportunity to score. If a point guard shoots the ball from down the court, his team will most likely lose the game. Point guards rarely get any glory. We work our buns off running from base line to base line, but the crowds don't applaud legwork.

Just as it is the point guard's duty to sacrifice to help his team win, it is the husband's responsibility to promote the welfare of his wife and children before himself.

THE WIFE'S JOB DESCRIPTION

A wife enjoys a challenging position in marriage. According to Scripture, she brings a unique blend of submission and respect to the husband-wife relationship. (Husbands, don't skip this section thinking it has nothing to do with you. In fact, this is just as much for you as it is for your wife.)

The wife is instructed to "honor" her husband. (See Eph. 5:21.)

Nowhere in the Bible is a woman told to "love" her husband. Why is that? Because loving comes more naturally to a woman. Bestowing honor, on the other hand, is a response most women have to work at developing.

Giving honor is not an emotion; it requires an act of the will. Even if you feel your husband is not worthy of your respect, you are still commanded to honor him. Why? Because he is your husband. You honor the position he holds in the family. We may not always respect the person who holds the office of president of the United States, but we must still honor the position.

If a wife bestows honor on her husband — whether he deserves it or not — a man will usually "rise to the occasion." Sometimes all it takes is a verbal affirmation like, "Honey, I really appreciate how hard you work to provide for us."

A wife should be her husband's cheerleader. Men love to be applauded when they do something special. If a wife wants to get flowers (or jewelry or whatever) every birthday, all she has to do is make a big deal the first time he brings them home. Then she'll get roses for the rest of her life!

A man needs to be honored by his wife. He won't tell you that because of his pride, but deep down

No man can tell whether he is rich or poor

by turning to his ledger. It is the heart that

makes a man rich.

Henry Ward Beecher (1813–1887)

inside men have a God-given yearning for honor.

How does a wife show honor? "Honor Christ by submitting to each other. You wives must submit to your husband's leadership in the same way you submit to the Lord" (Eph. 5:21-22). *The Message* translation puts it this way: "Wives, understand and support your husbands."

What does it mean to "understand and support"? In their book, *The Hidden Value of a Man,* Gary Smalley and John Trent define submission:

> In Ephesians 5, before wives are called to submit, we read, "Submit to one another out of reverence for Christ." In Greek, the original language of the New Testament, being "subject to" another person was actually a military term. It's a word that speaks of support, voluntary allegiance, and cooperation. It leaves room for creativity and even questioning while maintaining a high commitment. It carries with it none of the damaging misconceptions of high control or manipulations but instead connotes teamwork and mutual respect.
>
> For a wife, submission involves responding to her husband's leadership "as to the Lord" — not as an inferior, but as one committed to a mutual goal that is worthy of her life.[2]

Unity is the result of becoming one: Leadership is provided by the husband, and the wife submits to a plan that is mutually agreed upon. Although we have outlined the husband's and wife's job descriptions independently, in reality they cannot be separated. If one mate fails to faithfully fulfill God's commands, unity breaks down and the marriage relationship suffers.

MISSION POSSIBLE

One day I caught the end of "The Oprah Winfrey Show" and heard Oprah say, "I never got into this business to make money. I got into this business to make a positive impact on this world. The money just happened to be a result of what I have done." That is quite a statement coming from one of the richest women in the world.

Surprisingly, the majority of companies that survive economic ups and downs do not remain afloat because they are driven by the need to make a profit. No, there is a more profound reason. These companies endure because they make a contribution to the world.

In 1891, George Merck decided to start a company that would help cure sickness. At the time, he did not have a single product to sell — but he had a vision.

This was Merck's mission statement: "We are in the business of preserving and improving human life. All of our actions must be measured by our success in achieving this goal."

The Merck Company demonstrated a purpose by the motives behind the decision-making. For example, in Third World countries over a million people were losing their eyesight to "River Blindness." This horrible disease, caused by a parasitic worm that swarms through body tissue and eventually invades the eyes, leads to painful blindness.

The Merck Company saw a need and developed a drug to cure the disease. With a potential market of over a million people, they could have profited greatly from sales of their drug. There was only one problem. Neither the people nor their bankrupt governments could afford to purchase the drug that could eliminate "River Blindness."

In keeping with their mission statement, the Merck Company elected to give the drug away free. The company even handled all the distribution at their own expense so that the drug would indeed get to the million people who needed it.

When asked why they elected to develop and give the drug away at the company's expense, the chief executive of Merck Company, P. Roy Vagelos, said "Above all, let's remember that our business success means victory against disease and help to humankind."[3]

When you got married, did you have a business plan, an employee handbook, or an orientation into the business of marriage?

Many couples get married because "we are in love and that's all that matters." Wonderful! But it takes more than romance to make a marriage fulfilling and meaningful.

Like the Merck Company, marriage needs a "mission statement" that spells out family values that will not be compromised for any reason or at any price. Your mission statement should be the driving force to a fulfilling and meaningful marriage.

Most couples have a mission statement; they just don't know it. Why? Because it is unspoken and never acknowledged.

In marriage, many men and women who "tie the knot" do so with the attitude, "How much can I get out of this?"

What are the goals of your marriage? Is it to have kids, have a good time, or stay together until retirement so you won't have to travel alone in your Winnebago?

Husband and wife do not necessarily need to have the same purpose or mission in life (although that is the ideal), but they do need a congruent set of values upon which the marriage is based. These values actually will become the "manual" for your marriage.

Every lasting and worthwhile endeavor must be based on a statement of purpose. When a group of men started the United States of America, they composed a document called the Declaration of Independence and signed it. That document became the driving force behind the American dream of liberty, freedom, and the pursuit of happiness. Your manual will keep your marriage focused on the goals and purposes you want to achieve in the years ahead.

ONE HEART, ONE MIND, ONE PURPOSE

What do the Declaration of Independence, a company manual, and a family business handbook have in common? They all produce the same result — unity.

The brave men who signed the Declaration of Independence were all unified in their purpose to start a nation that would be governed by the people. The women and men who went to work for the Merck Company and signed their value statement were in unity. What were the results of these two endeavors? Longevity and success.

The United States of America has become the most powerful country in the world. At the signing of the Declaration of Independence, however, the 13 original colonies were considered little more than a rag-tag bunch of farmers. Unified in principle and purpose, they banded together to fight for their freedom.

The employees of the Merck Company — from delivery drivers to upper management — are all in agreement of "preserving and improving human life." Every day each individual in the company shows up at work with the goal of making a contribution to society.

Marriage requires the same commitment of purpose and unity. Following is our family's mission statement.

GIBSON'S INC. MISSION STATEMENT

"The earth is the Lord's and everything in it" (Ps. 24:1;NIV).

RUNNING THE FAMILY BUSINESS

We acknowledge that God owns 100 percent of everything and we are to be good managers of His resources. We are to be responsible for living within the amount He gives us and to give to the church and needy.

Giving: "Honor the Lord with your wealth, with the firstfruits of all your crops" (Prov. 3:9;NIV).

We will give a minimum of 10 percent of our income to the church and the Great Commission.

Planning: "The plans of the diligent lead to profit as surely as haste leads to poverty" (Prov. 21:5;NIV). "We should make plans — counting on God to direct us" (Proverbs 16:9).

We will plan the present and future diligently with what God has entrusted to us.

Contentment: "One hand full of rest is better than two fists full of labor and striving after wind" (Eccles. 4:6;NAS). "He who loves money shall never have enough" (Eccles. 5:10).

We will live within our means with the resources God gives us and with our focus on Christ because He is our only source of contentment.

Kind and Loving: "Be kind to each other, tender-hearted, forgiving one another, just as God has forgiven you because you belong to Christ" (Eph. 4:32).

We will resolve our differences in a kind and loving way without letting the sun go down on our anger.

Debt: "The rich rule the poor, so the borrower is servant to the lender" (Prov. 22:7). "The wicked borrow and do not repay" (Ps. 37:21;NIV).

We will not take on any debt outside of our home mortgage. We want to become debt-free so God can use us any way He pleases to pursue His plan for us.

Faith: "Faith is being sure of what we hope for and certain of what we do not see" (Heb. 11:1;NIV). "If you have faith as small as a mustard seed, you can say to this mountain, 'Move from here to there' and it will move. Nothing will be impossible for you" (Matt. 17:20-21;NIV).

God will always be our provider, and we will trust Him to provide for us.

Distractions: "The attractions of this world and the delights of wealth, and the search for success and lure of nice things come in and crowd out God's message" (Mark 4:19).

God will be at the center of our lives, and we will live our life according to what He has planned for us.

CREATING A "VALUE STATEMENT"

Like the CEO of a company, a husband should have a business plan in alignment with the family's value statement. What is a value statement? A value statement includes two elements:

1. What you are about.
2. What you do.

The Merck Company value statement reads this way: "We are workers in industry who are genuinely inspired by the ideals of advancement of medical science, and of service to humanity." In other words, they are scientists in the business of serving humans through their services.

Underneath their value statement is a list of values that need to be followed for them to experience success. Here are a few examples.

• Honesty and integrity.
• Science-based innovations, not imitation.
• Unequivocal excellence in all aspects of the company.
• Profit, but profit from work that benefits humanity.

Just as businesses benefit from having a value statement, marriages can also improve their relationship and fulfill their goals by having a marriage value statement.

You may think that value statements are a new concept. Actually, the ancient Book of Proverbs in the Bible makes this observation: " Where there is no vision, the people are unrestrained, But happy is he who keeps the law" (Prov. 29:18;NAS). Even before the birth of Christ, people knew the value of having a vision and purpose in life. Why? Because if you don't know where you are going, you are lost.

The great theologian, Alice in Wonderland, says: "If you don't know where you are going, any road will get you there."

What will a written value statement do for your family? Here are some of the benefits:

- Clarifies the direction of your marriage.
- Gives us a reference to refer to in the future.
- Reduces conflicts.
- Provides security.
- Reduces stress.

What goes into writing a family value statement?

It should include the purpose and mission of your marriage. In your statement you want to think about what you want your marriage to communicate to your friends, neighbors, family members, church, community, etc.

Well-known management consultant Peter Drucker makes this suggestion to business owners who want to know how their business is doing. Ask yourself two questions, "What is our business?" and "How is business?"

As a married couple, you need to ask yourself similar questions: What do we want to share with the world? How are we going to measure our success?

If you have children, you may want to include them

THERE ARE A THOUSAND WAYS TO WEALTH BUT ONLY ONE WAY TO HEAVEN.

JOHN LOCKE (1632–1704)

in writing your family's value statement. They will probably have unique ideas that you may not have considered. Then, whether you are together as a family or separated by school or college or camp, your kids will know what you expect from them.

The common denominator for everything you do will be based upon your purpose statement.

DEVELOPING A FAMILY BUSINESS HANDBOOK

After your purpose statement has been created, the next step is to develop regulations for the Family Business Handbook. This handbook will serve as a guideline for all family decisions. Be sure to include Bible verses to validate your points.

I have listed examples with verses you may want to include in your handbook.

- Relationship with God: Matthew 6:33, Galatians 2:20
- Commitment: Mark 10:7
- Wisdom: James 1:5
- Tithe: Exodus 22:29
- Taxes: Matthew 22:21
- Debt: Psalms 37:21
- Spending: Luke 12:15
- Planning: Proverbs 17:24
- Communication: James 1:19
- Investing: Proverbs 21:5
- Providing: 1 Timothy 5:8
- Children: Ephesians 6:4
- Work: Colossians 3:23-24
- Anger: Ephesians 4:26

All these principles — and more which you can tailor to your family's uniqueness — will become the driving force of your marriage and family.

For example, April 15 arrives and you have to pay $1,500 to the IRS in taxes. As much as you don't want to pay, you do so because your family handbook says, "Give to Caesar what is Caesar's." This guideline leaves no question as to whether or not you should pay.

The handbook creates harmony and security in your marriage because you have the security of knowing every family member is on the same playing field as a team.

If all marriages had a value statement detailing the goals for their marriage, the divorce rate would drop dramatically. After all, research shows that 56 percent of all divorces are related to financial tension in the home.

A Family Business Plan eliminates that tension because it tells you what to do. If a question comes up about spending, you can review your handbook to see what guidelines you have set.

You may have decided that if either mate spends more then $25, he/she must consult with the other mate. This kind of mutual arrangement eliminates conflict. Why? Because there will be no big-ticket surprises!

By determining your own values and creating a value statement, you will strengthen your relationship. Written goals and predetermined expectations provide boundaries within which you can both operate safely. When husband and wife know the other partner is committed to the same goals for their marriage, confusion and conflict evaporate. Misunderstanding — or misinterpretations — can be resolved with one statement: Go get the family handbook!

Congratulations! You and your mate have mapped out the direction you want your marriage and finances to take.

Before you can get started down the road to achieving your family goals, however, you must first pinpoint your current location. That means "back to the present." After all, how can you know where you're going if you don't know where you are?

CHAPTER SEVEN

WHERE ARE YOU?

IMAGINE that you and your mate have driven out of the city to enjoy a weekend of camping in the forest. You are excited to be in an area of the country you have never visited before and can't wait to go exploring.

After setting up the tent and securing your campground, the two of you decide to take a nature walk.

"Look at those trees!" you say to your spouse. "I've never seen any that tall in our neck of the woods."

"Wow!" she responds as you both gaze up at the mountains. "God sure knew what He was doing when He created this place!"

After walking for a while beside a river, you come to a ravine bridged by a natural rock formation. As you cross the ravine, your foot suddenly slips and you fall on your head, knocking yourself unconscious.

Your wife begins to panic. "I've got to get help! But I don't know the way to our campsite. Maybe Tom brought a compass," she tells herself while frantically searching your backpack and pockets.

No compass. No map.

"If only I had paid more attention to the details along the way, I could find my way back. Now I'm lost with nothing to direct me! What will I do now?"

In this situation, what do you need to get back to safety? You need:

1. To find out where you are (your current location).
2. To know where you want to go (back to safety).
3. To plan a way to get to your desired destination (map).

The same procedure applies to your financial situation. You may feel stranded without any hope of ever getting back to square one, but don't despair. If you follow the steps outlined in this chapter, you will at least know where you are — and be on your way out of the financial wilderness and into a place of safety and security.

It is ironic that on Amelia Earhart's last flight, she was at the peak of her fame. She knew who she was in terms of goals accomplished and where she wanted to go in life. How tragic that certain assessments had not been made that would allow her to see an island landmark on her bid to fly around the world.

In one of her last transmissions, it was clear she was unable to spot her landmarks. And landmarks — past and present — are vital in determining whether you are on track or have veered off course.

Sometimes, we want to jettison what we perceive to be a cropduster existence for the luxury of a jet. In answering the question, "Where are you?" I want us to focus on this scenario with a slightly different twist: "Are you going to fly a cropduster or a jet for God?"

Jesus said that we are to seek first the kingdom of God and, later, earthly blessings will come. Your current motivation — to serve God or not — will determine what kind of pilot you are going to be. Are you going to fly by the book or take off on your own?

Before proceeding on your journey, you need to pinpoint your current financial condition. You can't make progress if you don't know how much money you have and how it is spent. Over 60 percent of couples have no idea where their money goes.

A MOUNTAIN OF DEBT?

Not long after Warren and Traci were married, they received devastating news: "Traci has a physical condition that will prevent her from getting pregnant," the doctor said.

For that reason, they decided it would be a waste of money to pay the added expense of maternal insurance. The doctor, however, was wrong, and Traci did get pregnant.

Considered a high-risk expectant mother, Traci was required to have a specialist monitor her pregnancy and perform a C-section at the delivery. Without insurance coverage for her treatment, the couple faced tremendous medical bills.

"I don't care how much she costs," Warren told his wife. "Our baby girl is worth every penny!"

The hospital and doctor expenses left them deep in debt with no money to meet some of their basic needs. Warren began using credit cards to buy the things they couldn't afford.

As they got deeper into debt, the bill collectors began to call.

"You've got to do something!" Traci demanded. "I can't take the stress any longer!"

"What can I do?" Warren shouted back. "Do you want to declare bankruptcy?"

"I don't care what you do!" Traci screamed. A few days later, she took the baby and left her husband.

Warren, depressed and looking for answers, began attending church. During our Sunday school class, he shared his heartache and financial troubles.

"I feel like I'm climbing Mt. Everest!" he told us.

Afterward, I approached him and said, "I would love to help you and Traci get back together and eliminate this monster of debt that has torn you apart."

A few days later, he brought all his bills in a shoe box and dumped them on the table. "Here it is," he said, "Mt. Everest!"

If you have ever watched any documentaries about expeditions up Mt. Everest, you are aware of the complicated planning and extensive preparation such a venture requires.

Still, no matter how high, every mountain is climbed in the same way: One step at a time.

Warren and Traci needed a step-by-step plan to get to the top.

PLANNING TO SUCCEED

One of the greatest leaders and planners of all time took a group of discouraged, defeated people and managed to pull off an impossible building project in 52 days. His name was Nehemiah, and his experiences are recorded in the Bible.

After many years in exile, the Jews had returned to Jerusalem from Babylon to find that the city walls and gates had been destroyed during the enemy's takeover.

Nehemiah, a Jewish scholar who held an important position in the court of the Babylonian king, was unaware of the situation in Jerusalem. When a friend came to visit, he told Nehemiah, "Things are not good; the wall of Jerusalem is still torn down, and the gates are burned" (Neh. 1:3).

Deeply burdened, Nehemiah began to pray and fast for his people. Through prayer and the consent of the king, Nehemiah began his journey to Jerusalem to help them rebuild the walls and gates of the city.

Three days after arriving in Jerusalem, Nehemiah sneaked out to survey the wreckage. After carefully examining what needed to be done, Nehemiah approached the Jewish leaders with a plan for rebuilding the city walls and gates.

NOTHING IS MORE
TERRIBLE THAN
ACTIVITY WITHOUT
INSIGHT.

THOMAS CARLYLE (1795–1881)

When he announced the strategy for rebuilding, the people enthusiastically replied, " 'Good! Let's rebuild the wall!" And so the work began' (Neh. 2:18).

Almost immediately, the construction crews were ridiculed by a group of whiners who told them their goal was impossible. Nehemiah, however, would not be dissuaded from his plan of action and refused to let anything stand in his way. (He probably had the temperament of a lion/beaver.)

With his leadership abilities, Nehemiah supervised, encouraged, and managed the people while dealing with the opposition at the same time. Using his organizational talents, he was able to survey, plan, and stick to the rebuilding schedule. Under God's direction, Nehemiah led the people to successfully rebuild the walls and gates in 52 days.

What can we learn from Nehemiah about successful planning procedures? Plenty.

During my meetings with Warren and Traci, I took them through the "Rebuilding the Wall" steps that had worked for Nehemiah.

1. Pray at every step of the process.

Nehemiah continually consulted God for direction and help. He prayed after he heard of the disaster, before he approached the king, during the planning, and when he spoke to the Jews and others. Nehemiah always sought God's wisdom first.

Did you know that God wants us to come to Him for help? "Call to me, and I will answer you, and I will tell you great and mighty things, which you do not know" (Jer. 33:3;NAB). Our Heavenly Father promises to help us find the solutions to our problems.

I explained this to Warren and Traci, and we prayed together, asking God to guide us in a direction that would put them on the right path.

Then I asked, "What are the 'holes' in your wall?"

Without offering any excuses, Warren immediately responded, "Overspending, credit card debt, not having enough money to pay all the bills, not providing for the future. I need God's help in all of these areas."

When seeking God's guidance for a financial problem, it is important to be specific.

2. Survey and think through your plan.

"A wise man thinks ahead; a fool doesn't, and even brags about it!" (Prov. 13:16).

Nehemiah first went out at night to inspect the rubble. When his survey was completed, he put a plan together to build the wall and gates step by step.

Warren and Traci's biggest "hole in the wall" was their credit card debt. Although the amount appeared to be insurmountable, I suggested, "Start a pro-active plan that will enable you to chip away at your debts."

Then I gave them the same plan outlined in chapter 9, "How to Get Rid of Debt."

3. Establish a goal.

Nehemiah set large goals, but he was able to achieve them because he divided each section of the wall into short-term goals. Each group of people had a different task and was responsible for completing it.

If your "hole in the wall" is like Warren's, you, too, are spending too much and not leaving enough money to pay your bills. I would tell you what I told Warren, "Establish a budget." (I call it a spending plan — as you will see in chapter 8.)

4. Set a deadline.

Nehemiah had to get the job done before his leave of absence from the king expired and before the people became discouraged.

Without a deadline, you don't have goals. All you have is wishful thinking. Deadlines turn dreams into goals. This is the area that gives your planning strength. Without dates for goals to be completed, you have nothing more than words on paper.

I told Warren and Traci, "Set a specific date to complete your debt reduction plan and to finalize your budget."

"How about next week?" Traci suggested, eager to get things rolling.

5. Anticipate the problems.

Nehemiah could see potential disasters before they occurred. He began by scouting the wreckage at night so no one would know why he was in Jerusalem. By devising his rebuilding strategy in advance, he was able to thwart the resistance of his enemies before he started the project.

"Since you have a tendency to overspend, how could you prevent potential problems?" I asked Warren and Traci.

"Well," Traci began, "we could avoid going to the mall."

"I could cut up all our credit cards," Warren added.

"Those are good strategies," I explained, "but if you are serious, you need to make additional sacrifices to help eliminate further conflicts between you."

6. Calculate the cost.

Nehemiah knew that leaving the comfort of the king's palace to take on such a massive project in a hostile environment would be a stressful and unappreciated effort. With strength and guidance from God, Nehemiah was able to accomplish his God-given task.

Finally, I told Warren and Traci, "Nothing done halfway is ever successful. If you are serious about improving your marriage relationship and getting your finances in order, you must put 100 percent of your effort into this project. It won't be easy, but with God's help, I know you can do it."

Nehemiah put hard work and all his energy into repairing the "holes in the wall." That's what it will take from you.

"Everything has a price tag attached," I told them. "To set goals and devise a plan is great, but putting your plan into action is the most difficult step."

KEPT IN THE DARK

Since Kathy's husband was a registered Certified Financial Planner, she allowed him to control their finances. Using his expertise as a cover, Bob hurriedly rushed her to sign their tax returns every year, "I've done all the work. All you need to do it sign it."

For 27 years Kathy knew nothing about their financial affairs because she trusted her husband to manage everything. When Bob was on his deathbed with terminal cancer, their daughter, a financial analyst, helped prepare her parents' tax returns.

"I'm finding things you're not going to believe," the daughter told Kathy. "Dad is in over his head, and you've got a problem."

Curious to discover the truth, Kathy decided to invade her husband's domain. Riffling through his papers, she found he had accumulated debts, IOUs, and mysterious partnerships.

After sorting out his financial dealings, Kathy calculated that her husband had many outstanding debts and only $175 in his checking account. Two weeks later Bob passed away. Instead of leaving Kathy with a secure financial future, she was forced to get a job to pay her husband's debts and earn an income for herself.

This incident, unfortunately, is not uncommon. Many times a spouse dies, and the other has no knowledge of their financial condition.

Like the hikers lost in the wilderness without a compass, many couples have no idea how much money they have in the bank or what they owe. Without these important signposts, you cannot crawl out of the ravine and return to safety.

You and your mate need to empty your pockets and wallets, surrender your checkbooks, and collect all your bills. Put all your "cards" on the table — literally — and take stock.

Then you can pinpoint your position on the money map.

YOUR FINANCIAL CHECKUP

With God's wisdom and help, Nehemiah succeeded in rebuilding the walls and gates of Jerusalem. As you set out on your journey to rebuild the financial structure of your home and marriage, start — as did Nehemiah — at the place where you find yourself today.

First, identify any "holes in the wall" or areas of weakness that must be rebuilt or made stronger.

Although her final flight ended tragically, Amelia Earhart made sure the sleek Electra she'd been given had been upgraded to give her the best possible chance to succeed on her around-the-world flight. In taking her "final checkup," Earhart had engineers modify the plane and add fuel tanks. She was responsible enough to take all necessary precautions.

A financial checkup can be compared to a physical checkup. It may be painful, but you are willing to endure the discomfort to determine the truth about your condition.

The following inventory, taken from Ron Blue's book,

Mastering Your Money, will reveal your financial condition.[1] By asking the following four questions, you will begin to develop a financial summary of your marriage. This is the first step to finance-proofing your marriage.

1. What do I owe?

The majority of Americans owe someone something. Overall, our nation owes trillion of dollars.

To have financial peace in your marriage, debts need to be controlled. In a later chapter, I will share how you can get out of debt and stay out. For now you need to determine who your creditors are, how much you owe each of your creditors, and the interest rate on each loan or credit card.

Creditor	Balance Owed	Monthly Payment	Interest rate
1.			
2.			
3.			
4.			
5.			

2. What do I own?

Most couples not only don't know what they owe, they don't even know what they own.

Heed this warning from the Wisdom of Solomon: "Riches can disappear fast. And the king's crown doesn't stay in his family forever — so watch your business interests closely" (Prov. 27:23).

For the most part, men would rather live in the dark than see

ONE-HALF OF
KNOWING WHAT
YOU WANT IS
KNOWING WHAT
YOU MUST GIVE UP
BEFORE YOU GET IT.
SIDNEY COE HOWARD (1891–1939)

their net worth spelled out in black and white. Wives need to be sensitive to their husbands' vulnerability in this area.

Keep the lines of communication open so you can both get a realistic picture of your assets. This exercise is well worth the time it takes, since this list will come in handy when you apply for a mortgage or make up a will. Following is a net holdings worksheet to help you take inventory of your belongings.

NET HOLDINGS WORKSHEET

Income: (money you receive)
Wages: husband
Wages: wife
Dividends
Dividends
Interest
Interest
Real Estate
   Rent
   Other
Other
TOTAL A:_____

Assets: (cash, possessions you own)
Checking account
CD account
Money market account
Marketable securities
   (mutual fund, stocks, bonds)
Cash value — life insurance
Business
Real Estate
Antiques, jewelry, etc.
IRAs - 401K
Loans receivable
Other
TOTAL B:_____
TOTAL A:_____ (add)
   TOTAL A & B_____

Liabilities (people, organizations you owe)
Home mortgage
Car loans
Bank loans
Credit card
Hospital
Gas card
Department store
Personal loans payable
Others
   TOTAL:_____
   TOTAL A & B:_____(subtract)
NET WORTH (where you are):_____

3. How much am I spending?

To gain control of your finances, you need to have a handle on how much you are spending each month.

You have probably made trips to the ATM machine and walked away with a wallet full of twenties. Within a few days, however, the well-stocked wallet is empty. Where did it all go?

To answer that question, why not take one month and keep a record of all your cash expenses? One easy way to do this is to ask for and keep a receipt for everything you and your mate purchase with cash. Put them in an envelope that you keep in the car, then take an inventory of all your purchases at the end of the month.

- How much do you spend eating out — or for pizza delivery?
- Are you buying more junk food instead of "real" food at the supermarket?
- Is your gas tank getting filled up every other day because you're always on the go?
- Do you have to patronize the most expensive hairdresser in the city?
- Do the kids need to wear designer clothes?

Once you know where your cash is going, take a moment and monitor your regular spending. Look through your checkbook register and identify everything that is not an absolute necessity. Write them in a list and then agree together on what you can live with — and without.

- How often do you use that gym membership?
- Do you pay someone to mow your yard and clean your house while you vegetate in front of the television?
- Do you subscribe to newspapers and magazines you never have time to read?
- How often do leftovers spoil in the fridge because you ate at fast-food restaurants all week?

Are you spending money for things that are unnecessary or go unused? These are questions you need to ask yourself.

In a later chapter I will outline a method that will help you control your spending without feeling squeezed by a budget.

4. How strong are my safety nets?

All of us at some time in our lives will go through unplanned events like death, disability, sickness, unemployment, and more. Hopefully, not all these things will happen to you. Still, you need to be prepared for these kinds of financially draining circumstances.

That means you need insurance:

- Health Insurance
- Dental and Vision Insurance
- House or Apartment Insurance
- Disability Insurance (if you are self-employed)
- Car Insurance
- Life Insurance

Determine which policies you have and which ones you need. In some cases, you may have too much insurance. It may be cheaper to set aside a certain amount every month for dental expenses than to pay a monthly premium. That, of course, depends on the size of your family. The point is: Get coverage only for what you truly need.

I encourage both of you to seek a qualified insurance professional to determine what you and your family need.

Ron Blue's books, *Mastering Your Money* and *Storm Shelter,*[3] cover this topic in detail and will answer most of your questions.

THE BEGINNING OF THE END

After several meetings with Warren and Traci, we reached Step Six of the "Rebuilding the Wall" process: Calculate the cost.

At that point, they made a decision: "We're going to give 100 percent of our energy to becoming debt-free."

Immediately they set up a debt reduction plan and sold one of their cars.

"I can easily drop Warren off at work and pick him up," Traci — a stay-at-home mom — proposed. "After all, his office is only three miles away."

Although it took them three years, this couple is now debt-free.

"If we hadn't learned the life-saving principles found in God's Word," Warren told me, "we would have made two trips to the courthouse — one for a bankruptcy hearing and the other for divorce proceedings!"

As you — like Warren and Traci — work your way toward

financial freedom, don't forget the most valuable lesson learned from that great man Nehemiah: Consult God for His guidance at every juncture.

I hope the inventory of your debts, assets, and spending found in this chapter has given you a better idea of your financial "place on the map." If so, you, too, can begin to prepare for the future.

Now that you know where you are, it's time to ask the question that causes 90 percent of all marital arguments: Where did all the money go?

Finding the answer to that question doesn't have to be a tedious job; it *can* be an exciting adventure. In the next chapter, you will learn the method Kari and I used — a process that minimized financial conflict and maximized marital harmony. Who could ask for anything more?

CHAPTER EIGHT
A SPENDING PLAN
WITH A PURPOSE

IF YOU are like me, the "B" word — budget — ranks right up there with dieting and root canals!

Whenever I mention the need for a budget, people will often respond with, "Just bury me now! What fun is life with a budget?"

You probably think it means you can't go anywhere, buy anything, or even sleep because you're worried about The Budget!

A budget, I admit, does place certain restrictions on unlimited spending. A budget used correctly, however, can be the best vehicle for getting where you want to go.

First, let's get rid of the word *budget*. Budget seems so confining and restricting. Instead, let's use "spending plan." A spending plan already sounds more upbeat, probably because it includes the word that most of us like most — *spending* (as in money).

For any endeavor, big or small, you must have a plan. I must have a plan. We can't hope to blindly fly in and out of a fog. Money management follows the same principle. When you decide to pilot your marriage with a spending plan, you are taking control of the wheel by assuming responsibility. This tends to ensure a good flight.

Most marriages have a spender and a saver. This double-barreled approach, however, can be more than dangerous — it can kill a budget quicker than you can pull the trigger.

My brother in-law, who is a saver, married a woman who is a spender. When it came time for them to reach a compromise, he decided to become a spender. If you ask him why, he answers, "Her ways were a lot more fun!"

Spending money is always more fun than saving, but the reason for a budget is to strike a balance between spending and saving.

Let's look at the positive aspects of a spending plan:

• A spending plan allows you to do anything you want to do — as long as it is included in your plan.

• A spending plan helps you decide *how* to spend your money. You are in control of where your money goes. If friends ask you if you would like to go to the opera and the tickets will cost $45 a piece, it's easy to say, "No, thank you."

• A spending plan eliminates having to say, "I can't afford it." Instead, a spending plan enables you to say, "I have other things I want to spend my money on."

When I was about eight years old, I left the house to visit a friend who lived several streets up from us. Back in those days I rarely wore shoes, so I took off in my bare feet.

After playing, I proceeded to walk back home. When I came to our block, I noticed men working on our street spreading some kind of black stuff.

Since my house was right on the corner, I only had to cross one street. Without knowing what the black stuff was, I put one foot out. At first I didn't feel anything, but halfway across my feet began to burn. They burned so bad I didn't know what to do next.

I zoomed across the rest of the street barefooted and into our yard. Painfully limping over to the outside faucet, I let the water cool down my feet. When I felt some relief, I looked at my feet and noticed they were covered with blisters.

Eventually my mom came out and exclaimed, "Oh my goodness! You walked in hot tar!"

Years later, I once again "walked in hot tar." Like many newlyweds, Kari and I learned early in our marriage about "the burn." After getting "burned" many times with our impulsive over-spending, we finally learned how to avoid the hot spots.

REWARDS AND CONSEQUENCES

What are some consequences of getting burned?

• Unwanted debt
• Impulsive spending
• Frustration
• Worry
• Increased spending

- Unwanted arguments
- Embarrassment
- Not being a good steward of God's property
- Anger

A spending plan, however, will get you from point A to point Z without being burned.

Couples who don't have a spending plan usually spend more than 33 percent of their income. After a while 33 percent can add up and leave you paying for it a long time.

Many couples go years without taking the time to commit to a spending plan. Why? Because they fear they won't be able to continue to live "in the manner to which they have become accustomed."

What they don't know is that a spending plan is just the opposite. A spending plan puts you in control of where you want your money to go. It actually puts wings to your finances and allows it to land at a predetermined destination instead of always viewing the same scenery day after day.

What are the rewards of a spending plan?

> Our plans miscarry because they have no aim. When a man does not know what harbor he is making for, no wind is the right wind.
>
> Lucius Annaeus Seneca (4 B.C.–A.D. 65)

- Allows you to live within your means.
- Provides security.
- Frees you to fulfill God's plan for your life.
- Provides for the future.
- Eliminates worry, frustration, and hurt feelings.
- Reduces conflicts.
- Provides guilt-free buying.
- Provides for your kids' future.

All these positive results look great, and you'd really like to see it work. "But," you say, "I have tried following a budget, and it has never worked."

You may have had a budget in effect for a brief time, but you reverted back to your old ways after a few months.

Why don't budgets work? They lack one crucial element.

THE MISSING LINK

Without one important ingredient, a spending plan will be absolutely worthless. It may work for a couple of months, but eventually it will lose its appeal.

Once you establish this "missing ingredient," you will find that a spending plan is simply a vehicle for getting you where you want to go. Actually, this principle will make you excited to have a spending plan. You will find yourself reviewing it to make sure you are on target.

Married couples disagree — not about the lack of money — but over not having any financial goals to measure their spending. Frustration over finances develops when there are no financial goals. Financial health is merely an illusion without predetermined goals.

The Consumer Federation of America and NationsBank conducted a national survey of 1,770 households and made a remarkable discovery: Families who had written a financial plan saved and invested twice as much as those who didn't.

Stephen Brobeck, executive director of the Consumer Federation of America, says, "We used to stress simply the importance of saving. But, as the result of our research, we now realize that planning itself leads to increased savings."[1]

Planning is done by setting goals. Without goals, there is no plan. Adriane Berg states, "The difference between a wish and a goal is a plan."[2]

A spending plan will become part of your life when it is designed around your goals. Whether your goal is to take a family ski vacation next year or to retire at age 60, a spending plan will turn that wish into reality.

STEPS TO EFFECTIVE GOAL SETTING

Let's look at six important steps that will help you set your goals and achieve them.

A Spending Plan with a Purpose

1. Consult God about your goals.

"We should make plans — counting on God to direct us" (Prov. 16:9).

When we don't consult God first and seek His direction, we risk making big mistakes. "And even when you do ask you don't get it because your whole aim is wrong — you want only what will give you pleasure" (James 4:3).

I admit I would love to have a Porsche 911, but it would be highly impractical on the farm. If I were to pray for one, I would be 99 percent sure I would never receive one. Why? A fast sports car out in farm country would only be for my pleasure.

God is not against our having nice things. If I needed a truck — which is very practical on a farm — I would be sure that God would provide.

Consulting God first is a must to effective goal-setting and planning. This is His promise to us: "Ask, and you will be given what you ask for. Seek, and you will find. Knock, and the door will be opened" (Matt. 7:7).

2. Write down your goals.

After prayerfully consulting God, He will put the right desires in your heart.

As a husband and wife, each of you should individually write down your own goals on a separate piece of paper. During this time allow yourself to really dream. Think of the rest of your life, and write down what you desire — everything from around-the-world vacations to providing for your kids and increasing your giving.

3. Prioritize your goals.

Each partner should review the list he or she has written and number the goals in order of importance.

Upon completion, both spouses should sit down and discuss the goals they have put down on their list. Allow each partner to share without any comments from the other. (Remember these are dreams.) You may be surprised to find that you have similar desires.

After each has shared his/her wish list, it is time to start making one list from both sets of goals. Start with the first goal and discuss it. Then proceed down the list until both mates are excited about the future.

4. Long-term/Short-term.

Using the new combined list of goals, you can begin to divide it into long-term and short-term goals.

Long-term goals take three years or longer to accomplish. For example: To be able to buy a retirement home next to the ocean in sunny Florida.

Short-term goals can be attained within three years. For example: To take the family to Disney World next summer.

Short-term can also be used to help you plan your long-term goals. For example: To start saving for your retirement home, you first need to set a short-term goal of paying off all debt.

You may want to type your list of goals and post it where the family can keep it in view. Then, if someone suggests buying a giant screen TV set, the others can remind him about the planned trip to Disney World.

Many times, unfortunate circumstances will arise, and it is tempting to lose focus. By having your goals written and kept visible, frequent reviews will keep everyone on the right path.

5. Turn it over to God.

Once the list is final and both husband and wife mutually agree on the goals, turn the list over to God. By consulting Him, He promises that His plan for us is good and not for harm.

"You can never please God without faith, without depending on Him. Anyone who wants to come to God must believe that there is a God and that He rewards those who sincerely look for Him" (Heb. 11:6). Look to God to direct you and guide you through your journey and trust Him.

6. Seek counsel.

Your goals may require the help of a professional to give you advice on turning your dreams into realities. Proverbs 15:22 says, "Plans go wrong with too few counselors; many counselors bring success." Notice that this verse does not say one counselor, but *many* counselors.

I have heard too many stories of couples losing their life's savings because they took the advice of a single financial planner. Always consult more than one counselor. You may consider discussing your plan with a certified accountant, tax lawyer, and certified financial planner.

CREATING A SPENDING PLAN

Now that you have determined your goals and know the direction you are headed, it is time to work on allocating where your money should go to help achieve those goals.

A Spending Plan with a Purpose

Before you can make an effective spending plan, you first need to gather some vital information.

1. Keep your value statement in mind.

In chapter 6 you learned how to write a financial value statement. Your spending plan should reflect the values and purposes set forth in that statement.

For example, if you stated that your family will follow the biblical principle of tithing, then the first item on your spending plan is: 10 percent of your income allocated to God.

2. Refer to your goals.

In the beginning of this chapter, we discussed the importance of drawing up effective family goals. When developing your spending plan, you should refer to your goal sheet to make sure you are in alignment with the goals you have set.

3. Know your income.

If you get paid weekly, bi-weekly, or monthly, you need to know your total income. This figure should reflect how much money — after taxes, benefits, etc. — you are actually bringing home. If your income varies (commissions, etc.) average out your income from the past six months and that will be the amount you use for a spending plan.

4. Determine your expenditures.

To make a spending plan, you need to have current knowledge of how you spend your money. If husband and wife work and eat lunch out at a restaurant each day, you need to know how much you both spend per week. If you get your hair cut every other month you need to know that total.

In order to create an accurate spending plan, you need to know how much money is spent on miscellaneous expenditures. Be as accurate as possible. If you guess, you will need to fine-tune your plan later. To get an accurate record of your spending, keep all cash and credit card receipts from all purchases or services that you receive in one month. (See the *List of Possible Expenditures* at the end of this chapter.)

5. Prioritize your expenditures.

After listing all your expenditures, you are now ready to prioritize them in order of importance.

Within each category, some items may be more important than others. For example: In the "Pets" category, taking Fido to the veterinarian is probably more important than paying to have him clipped and groomed.

HIS, HERS, AND OURS

In my research for this book, I came across many good spending plans and budget systems. All of them, however, had one drawback. The typical method for actually putting a spending plan into effect centered around one bank account and one checkbook.

Our sole purpose in this book, however, is to help married couples resolve their money conflicts. And nothing creates more confusion and conflict in a marriage than "the checkbook."

Reality tells us that the two people who use the checkbook — the husband and wife — are not always together when money is spent. As a result, some transactions do not get recorded. To make matters worse, neither spouse knows exactly how much money is in the account at any given time because both are writing checks.

Couples who use a one-account system constantly argue. How do I know? Because Kari and I used this method for the first three years of our marriage, and we experienced many checkbook "discussions." Neither of us ever had the right information to balance or keep track of our account.

In an effort to find a method that would reduce the confusion and keep us on track with our spending plan, I interviewed several couples. Those who had the least conflict over finances used a general system of checking. To learn more about this method, I decided to talk with the experts on money — bankers.

Bankers constantly deal with people who have problems with overdrafts and keeping their checking organized. Overall, the bankers had this advice for married couples: "Get two joint accounts — one is "his" and the other "hers.""

After hearing about this method, I did exactly as the bankers suggested. Since then, Kari and I have been basically conflict-free of checkbook discussions.

To get started with this method, you need to get two "free" checking accounts. Free checking is an account that will not charge you for maintenance or for carrying a low balance. This saves money since you won't be penalized if your account balance falls too low.

The two accounts need to be joint accounts with both husband and wife named on both accounts. This does not mean you are now independent of your mate or that you have your own money. The objective is to have a functional method for keeping your spending plan in line with your goals.

A SPENDING PLAN WITH A PURPOSE
MAKING THE SYSTEM WORK

Once you have your two joint accounts up and running with two separate checkbooks, you can begin to divide and conquer! Here's how to make the system work.

1. Decide how paychecks will be deposited.

Let's look at the two ways this can be done.

A. All checks are deposited into one account.

If you deposit all checks into one account, this helps keep the total consistent. It doesn't matter which account the money goes into as long as the other spouse has access to it.

One way to do this is through automatic transfer of funds from one account to the other's account. This is simple to set up.

First, add the total amount of each mate's responsibilities and have the funds transferred automatically by the bank to the other person's account.

An automatic transfer will keep the method consistent. If you deposit your paycheck on the 1st and 15th day of the month, you can have an automatic transfer of funds designated for the 2nd and 16th. Then you are only responsible for recording the transfer in your checkbook.

The first few months, you may want to call the bank to confirm that the transfer has been made.

B. Each spouse deposits his or her own paycheck into his or her account.

When both husband and wife work, they often want to deposit their individual salaries into their own account. This arrangement also works well as long as both mates consistently fulfill their payment responsibilities.

Many two-career couples find it easier to maintain separate accounts in order to keep track of business expenses and other job-related needs like clothes, parking, dry cleaning, day care, etc.

One couple has used this method successfully for several years. The husband, who is the main provider for the family, deposits his paycheck into his joint account. At the end of the month, he writes all the big bills — mortgage, car payment, utilities, etc., and pays for all the major family purchases, including groceries, eating out, etc.

His wife, who operates a small home-based business, deposits her income into her own joint account. After paying all her business-related expenses, she uses her profit for all the family "extras" — like piano lessons for their daughter and monthly window cleaning.

Since the wife does all the clothes shopping for the family, she keeps track of the department store bills and takes responsibility for paying them as well.

2. Divide the bill-paying responsibilities.

Once you have a detailed list of your monthly — or regular — expenses, you and your mate can decide who pays what.

Kari and I divide up the phone bill according to who is most responsible for the cost. I pay for the mobile phone service since I tend to use it the most. Kari pays the home phone bill since she makes the most toll calls. This method actually saves us money.

When the mate most responsible for the expenditure has to pay out of his or her account, he or she tends to try to keep costs down.

Some couples evenly divide up the bills. In some marriages, the wife pays for all cash-related expenses — groceries, gifts, eating out, etc. — while the husband prefers to take care of the monthly bills.

3. Each spouse is responsible for his or her bank account.

This means that the wife writes checks, records them in her check register, and keeps it in order. She also reviews the monthly statement and makes sure it balances. The husband does the same for his account.

THE GREAT THING IN THE WORLD IS NOT SO MUCH WHERE WE STAND, AS IN WHAT DIRECTION WE ARE MOVING.

OLIVER WENDELL HOLMES (1809–1894)

The other spouse should be available to help — especially if one mate is "numerically challenged." Overall, however, the responsibility for keeping the account up-to-date rests with the "owner."

Remember, if you bounce a check, it comes out of your account.

A Spending Plan with a Purpose

If this is your first try at creating a spending plan, I know it can be very tedious as well as depressing. Once you have listed all your obligations, it is not unusual to find there is no money left.

Do not get discouraged. If you have built up debts from the past, stay tuned and read the next chapter. There is hope.

FOLLOW-UP

Follow-up is the key to any successful venture.

For an Olympic athlete, it may be reviewing their last game with a coach and seeing what fundamentals need work. The athlete may realize he needs to work on the basics so he can improve for the next game.

A person trying to lose 15 pounds could benefit from a weekly follow-up with a partner to measure his or her progress. This is why Weight Watchers and other diet programs that regularly monitor weight loss are so successful. Without follow-up it is impossible to measure if you have made any progress.

Couples who have incurred a lot of debt or who spend beyond their means may need outside help from a trusted friend or a professional financial advisor to whom they are accountable. As in the examples mentioned above, follow-up meetings are key to keeping on track with your goals and mission.

Businesses constantly conduct meetings to measure progress and plan for the future. Yet we give little attention to marriage and family finance affairs.

Remember, your money and obligations go wherever you go. So give careful attention to the planning and progress of the spending plan you have developed for your family.

LIST OF POSSIBLE EXPENDITURES

Giving
- Church tithe
- Missionaries
- Charities

Savings
- Investment
    (college, etc.)
- Retirement (401k)
- Other

Debts
- Credit cards
- School loans
- Departments store
- Other

Housing
- Mortgage
- Rent

Utilities
- Electricity
- Water
- Gas
- Telephone (local,
    long distance)
- Cable TV
- Trash

Home Maintenance
- Yard
- Garden
- Maintenance

Food
- Groceries
- Business lunches
- Eating out
- Other

Clothing
- Husband
- Wife
- Children
- Laundry
- Dry Cleaning
- Other

Medical
- Doctor
- Dentist
- Prescriptions
- Eyeglasses
- Medical insurance
- Dental insurance
- Other

Transportation
- Car payment
- Gas
- Licensing
- Registration
- Oil/lube
- Tires
- Inspection
- Public transportation
- Parking
- Repairs
- Other

Gifts
- Birthdays
- Anniversaries
- Christmas
- Holidays (Mother's Day, etc.)
- Wedding
- Other

A Spending Plan with a Purpose

Entertainment
- Dates
- Family night
- Parties
- Clubs
- Shows (movies, plays, etc.)
- Video rentals
- Vacations

Recreation
- Gym fees
- Hobbies
- Sporting events
- Other

Household
- Furniture
- Appliances
- Linens
- Utensils
- Tools
- Hair products
- Toiletries

Pets
- Food
- Shots
- Veterinarian
- License
- Grooming

Personal Services
- Beauty salon
- Barber shop

Insurance
- Auto
- Home
- Life
- Disability
- Unemployment
- Property/casualty
- Renter
- Other

Taxes
- Federal
- State
- Social Security
- Other

Child Care
- Day care
- Baby-sitting
- Activities fees
- Other

Miscellaneous
- Alimony
- Child support

DANGER: DAD WITH CLIPPERS!

This chapter wouldn't be complete without another painful failure of my own making. (Keep in mind that it's possible to go overboard with a spending plan.)

Once upon a time, not so long ago, my son needed a haircut. He had fully recovered from the earlier, beauty salon fiasco.

Now in my full "spending plan mode," I looked Michael up and down and decided that I could give him a haircut and save money to boot. This idea came to me although I had no more training than an army barber.

Michael's response to my brainstorm was enthusiastically affirmative, so we marched outside after I found the clippers.

As I held the clippers in my hands, I noticed that they were for poodles, not humans — and specifically not for young boys. "Oh well." Throwing caution to the wind, I began.

After a few upward swipes, I noticed that there was not one even place on his head. To be frank, he had numerous bald spots.

Reacting as any immature boys would do, we ditched the clippers. "Go ahead and play!" I told Michael, who was eager to comply.

I headed in the opposite direction, keeping a lookout for Kari.

After some time, Kari saw Michael and shrieked, "What happened?"

Michael innocently replied, "Daddy gave me a haircut."

Needless to say, she requested an explanation. When I told her that my original goal had been to save money, she began laughing.

"I guess it was time for his summer haircut anyway," she said as she marched Michael to the car.

The trip to the salon drove home an important point for me: Don't "outspend-plan" your spending plan. You can end up costing yourself more money in the long run!

Remember, a spending plan is merely a vehicle to get you from your current location to your final destination — financial freedom. Too much of a good thing — like watching every penny — can become compulsive and take all the fun out of life. (Not to mention put your child's life in danger!)

At the same time, going overboard and spending every penny you make can put your marriage on "crash alert." Too many couples end up with smoke in the cockpit because they fail to put out the fire of debt before it consumes everything they own — including their relationship.

If you are already in over your head, the next chapter offers hope and practical ways to extinguish the biggest financial inferno you will ever face.

CHAPTER NINE

GETTING RID OF DEBT

ANOTHER trip to the mailbox rewards me with a personal letter, three direct mail ad pieces, an unsolicited catalog, and two credit card brochures pitching their latest incentives to get me into debt. In fact, I receive more credit card letters than I do personal letters!

Andersen Consulting says that in 1989 the average spender held 7 credit cards. Today, that purse or wallet carries 11.

Department stores, groceries stores, and even the U.S. Post Office are all eager to take your credit card. On a typical day, you can go grocery shopping, run by the local department store and pick up a new shirt, and then on your way home stop by the post office for stamps without spending a dime — at least until the bill shows up in the mail!

Every day brings some new reason to use the credit card and a new way to sink further into debt.

Newlyweds are the worst when it comes to debt. Why? Because they come to marriage with a lot of emotional and financial baggage.

• *The "honeymoon" debt.*

"I've been dreaming of a honeymoon in Hawaii since I was 12 years old. Since we don't have the money, let's charge it! After all, you only have one honeymoon." (Unfortunately, that's not always the case!)

• *The "inheritance" debt.*

The wife inherits her husband's school loan, and the husband inherits his wife's car loan. Before they even say, "I do," they are already thousands of dollars in debt.

I regularly meet couples who complain about the debt they have incurred over the years. My first question is always, "What are you going to do to get out?"

A typical reply includes a shrug of the shoulders followed by, "I don't know."

How can so many people get into debt and resign themselves to spending the rest of their lives in the "plastic hole"?

TAKEN BY SURPRISE

During Kari's pregnancy with our daughter Hannah, complications kept her in the hospital for 64 days. Meanwhile, I was balancing the demands of keeping Kari happy and entertaining our two-and-a-half-year-old son Michael.

Every Wednesday and on weekends, Michael would join me at the hospital to visit Mommy. Since Michael was not exactly the quiet visiting type, he required several "playtime breaks."

Michael loves to play with anything that has wheels, and what could be more fun at a hospital than a wheelchair? Pushing me around and running me into walls — and anything else he could find — came to be Michael's way of having fun.

One warm, sunny day I told him, "Let's play outside!"

I took my usual place in the wheelchair while Michael pushed me around. After we finished and were heading back inside, Michael suddenly flipped the wheelchair, and I went flying head over heels into the bushes by the entrance door.

Three nurses who had just gotten off work and were headed to the parking lot rushed to my rescue. "Are you all right?" they asked, checking to make sure I had no permanent damage.

Since the "accident" had happened near the hospital entrance, people from the lobby also streamed out to help. (I'm so lucky!)

"Let me help you back into your wheelchair," one of the nurses offered.

"No, no," I said sheepishly as I stood to my feet. "My son and I were just playing."

"Oh," she replied, staring at the little 35-pound boy who had just flipped a full-grown man out of a wheelchair.

Debt can do what Michael did to me — leave you flat on your face. If you're not watching it, debt can take you by surprise before you know what happened.

One way to get thrown off-balance is to co-sign a loan for a friend or relative. According to research conducted by banks, 50 percent of all co-signers end up making the payments. No wonder the Bible warns against this practice. "It is poor judgment to countersign another's note, to become responsible for his debts" (Prov. 17:18).

Co-signing a note puts you — and your credit — at tremendous risk. In fact, it ranks right up there with getting into a wheelchair pushed by a two year old! *You* usually end up the unsuspecting victim.

If you have co-signed for someone, get out of the situation as quickly as possible. Even if you have to swallow your pride and beg to be released from the note, do it immediately! (See Prov. 6:1-5.)

A MONEY-MAKING BUSINESS

Lending institutions are not simply being nice when they say, "Here is some money. Go out and buy something on us." Sure, they encourage us to use their money, but they plan to get it back — along with plenty more!

Loan companies and credit card corporations are in the business of making money. In 1996, the banking industry had a record profit of $52 billion.

How do they make so much money? They use a formula called "compounding interest."

For example, you buy a new car for $10,000 and borrow to pay for it at 12.5 percent over four years. After four years of payments of $265.80, you will have paid $12,758.40 for a car that is worth only $10,000.

Interest always works against you, making you "a servant to the lender" (Prov. 22:7). That is the consequence of unnecessary debt.

As a rule, all debt should be avoided if possible. Debt is permissible, however, in certain circumstances:

> • The item purchased is an asset with the potential to appreciate or produce an income. Example: A computer for your home-based business.
> • The value of the item equals or exceeds the amount owed against it. Example: An reliable car to drive to work.
> • The debt is so large the re-payment would put undue strain on the budget. Example: A mortgage on a house.

Going into debt to pay for a vacation or to buy a brand new car every year is financial suicide. Avoid debt whenever possible. If you do need a loan for the reasons noted above, shop wisely and, remember, you don't always have to buy the best of everything.

HOW TO GET OUT OF DEBT

By going into debt, you have already gambled against your future. God's Word teaches against such presumption:

> Come now, you who say, "Today or tomorrow we will go to such and such a city, and spend a year there and engage in business and make a profit." Yet you do not know what your life will be like tomorrow. You are just a vapor that appears for a little while and then vanishes away" (James 4:13-14;NAS).

If you really want to get out of debt and be financially free, I strongly encourage you and your spouse to start now. If you are waiting for "the right time" to start paying off your debts, forget it! The only right time is now — today, this moment!

Let's look at four steps you can take to get out of debt:

1. Make the decision.

To become debt-free you must make a decision: "I am *not* going to live above my means anymore."

After all, that's a biblical principle: "But godliness and contentment is great gain. For we brought nothing into the world, and we can take nothing out of it. But if we have food and clothing, we will be content with that" (1 Tim. 6:6-8;NIV).

WHO GOETH A BORROWING GOETH A SORROWING.

THOMAS TUSSER
(1524-1580)

2. Get rid of all hindrances.

Credit cards, cars loans, or anything you are making payments on that is not absolutely necessary. For example: computer, stereo, TV, furniture, appliances, etc.

3. Institute a game plan.

I call this method of debt eradication "Fireman's Elimination."

If you saw a house on fire, you would probably get a hose and start spraying down the smaller flames on the perimeter. You wouldn't rush into the burning building waving your hose in all directions, would you? No. You would put out the fire in one specific area and then work your way through to the larger flames.

Eliminating debt is the same. Start with the smallest debt and work your way to the bigger debt. In other words, put out the smallest fire first.

During my counseling sessions with Warren and Traci, I showed them how to eliminate their debts by conquering the blaze one hot spot at a time. You can apply these same steps to your situation.

1. Make a list of all the debts you owe along with the minimum payment for each debt and the interest.

(These are not the actual payments that Warren and Traci had to make. For this example, I have used simple numbers and not added interest into the payments.)

Debt	Balance	Payment	Interest
Gas Card	$75	$25	13%
Credit Card #1	$200	$30	21%
Credit Card #2	$400	$45	18%
Sears Card	$700	$60	13%
Hospital Bill	$1200	$130	7%
	$2575	$290	

2. Determine the total amount of debt you owe each month.

Using the examples given above, the total minimum monthly payments come to $290. That's the amount you will be paying every month until all your debts are paid.

3. Start by paying off the debt that has the lowest balance.

In the example given above, the $75 debt on the gas card is the smallest. With a minimum payment of $25, that's the debt you would pay off first.

4. When one debt is paid off, put the amount you were paying on that debt toward the next debt until all of it is paid.

The $25 monthly payment you were paying on the gas card will be put toward your next smallest debt — credit card #1. You would now begin to pay $55 to credit card #1 instead of $30.

The results of this systematic approach to debt reduction can be astounding — as this chart shows.

Payment Schedule

Owe	Month 1	2	3	4	5	6	7	8	9	
Gas card	25	25	25	done						
Cr. Card #1	30	30	30	55	55	done				
Cr. Card #2	45	45	45	45	45	100	75	done		
Sears card	60	60	60	60	60	60	85	160	95	done
Hospital	130	130	130	130	130	130	130	130	160	done
Total	290	290	290	290	290	290	290	290	255	done w/$35 left over

9 months = debt-free

After making the three final payments to the gas card, Warren and Traci were already experiencing some relief. Remember, they were also making regular monthly payments to their other creditors, so those were reduced, also.

"We're on our way!" Warren exclaimed. "I'm ready to take on the next debt — credit card #1."

"Just think" Traci added, "in two more months, we'll have that one paid off!"

In fact, their total debt was eliminated in less than 10 months, keeping them from paying additional interest.

The key to this method is not to take on any more debt during the paydown period.

"Keep out of debt and owe no man anything" (Rom. 13:8;Amp). That's good advice we would all be wise to follow.

As you apply the principles from this chapter and start putting out the fire of debt, you'll be well on your way to rescuing your financial freedom.

The real bonus comes from all that extra money you'll have at the end of each month! Now you are faced with an exciting predicament: What do I do with it?

We'll answer that question later, in chapter 11, where you will learn how to make the "compounding interest" that once worked *against* you work *for* you!

First, I want to share a truth that changed my life. Join me in chapter 10, as I explain the *Principles That Can Make or Break You.*

CHAPTER TEN
PRINCIPLES THAT CAN MAKE OR BREAK YOU

EVERY day I meet people who are struggling with money and possessions. Sometimes it's not the amount of money that concerns them, but the perceived need.

Are you worried about the unpaid bills covering your desk? "How am I going to pay all these?"

A new baby? Now there's an event full of financial challenges! Along with 21 years of providing clothes, haircuts, and braces comes the nagging question: How will I afford college tuition? Kids are great, but they are expensive — and take up a lot of room.

Maybe you've outgrown the house that served you well as newlyweds. Now two kids and a dog later, the closets are bursting at the seams and there's no place for the kids to play. "But a bigger mortgage would put us over the top!" you tell your wife.

Just about the time everything seems to be falling into place, God gives us another opportunity to learn to trust Him. In fact, money seems to be one His favorite topics.

In the Bible, God tells us more about money than heaven and hell combined. One out of every six verses in Matthew, Luke, and John deal with finances. Sixteen out of Christ's 38 parables focus on money. In all, there are over 2,000 Scripture verses that relate to financial principles.

Learning how to handle money properly poses one of life's toughest assignments. That must be why God often uses money to teach us His principles for daily living.

One day a young man from a wealthy family approached Jesus and asked, "Good master, what must I do to have eternal life?"

Jesus responded by quoting several of the commandments: "Don't kill, don't commit adultery, don't steal, don't lie, honor your father and mother, and love your neighbor as yourself."

The young man responded: "I've always obeyed every one of them. What else must I do?"

Jesus, however, could see into the heart of this young man who obviously had plenty of money, chariots, servants, and expensive clothes. "You're missing one important aspect of discipleship," Jesus answered. "Give it all up. Go and sell your possessions and give the money to the poor, and you will have treasure in heaven. Then, come and follow me."

The young man considered this idea for a moment but decided the price was too high. He turned and walked away sadly (see Matt. 19:16-26). That young man will never know what he missed. If he had said, "Yes!" and had sold his belongings and given the income to the poor, he would have received unbelievable treasures in heaven.

We need to ask ourselves that same penetrating question: Am I willing to follow Jesus Christ 100 percent?

To keep my heart — and my money — in perspective, I like to use this diagram:

G – God owns 100 percent of everything.
O – Owe God what is His.
D – Distractions: Beware!

Let's look at these three principles and how they relate to your money.

GOD OWNS EVERYTHING

When I was growing up, my brother used everything of mine. If I bought a new shirt, I would find the bag in my room and the shirt in my brother's closet. If I needed my car, there was a good chance it wouldn't be in the driveway. It really bothered me that my brother would take my stuff without asking permission.

God, on the other hand, has loaned out everything He has. Genesis 1:1 tells us: "In the beginning God created the heavens and the earth." Everything in this world — the trees, animals, plants, rocks, dirt, water, minerals — is God's property because they come from the things God created. He is the Creator and rightful owner of it all.

God also created man in His image (Gen. 1:27) to rule over "the fish of the sea and over the birds of the sky and over the cattle and over all the earth, and over every creeping thing that creeps on the earth" (Gen. 1:26;NAS).

Then in verse 28, God tells us to be "fruitful and multiply" (the one commandment we have been able to keep!), "subdue it; and rule over . . . every living thing that moves on the earth."

Now let's jump over to Genesis 2:15: "Then the Lord God placed the man in the Garden of Eden as its gardener, to tend and care for it."

When God created the earth, He "saw it was good" (Gen. 1:25;NIV). After the creation of man in Genesis 1:31: "God saw it was VERY GOOD." God created man in His image and delegated us to manage all the things on the earth.

What significance does this have for you and me? I am 100 percent in charge of managing God's resources, but I am the owner of nothing!

Before I could acknowledge that God is the absolute owner of everything, I was a slave to my possessions. By confessing that God owns 100 percent of everything, I become a steward of His possessions and property.

What is a "steward"? This is Webster's definition: "One who manages another's property, finances, or other affairs."

This is why Christ says:

> For unless you are honest in small matters, you won't be in large ones. If you cheat even a little, you won't be honest with greater responsibilities. And if you are untrustworthy about worldly wealth, who will trust you with the true riches of heaven? And if you are not faithful with other people's money, why should you be entrusted with money of your own? (Luke 16:10-12).

In other words, what you do with what you have now determines how much responsibility and wealth and money you will receive later.

What is Jesus trying to teach His disciples? I see three points that He is making:

1. Everything in this world belongs to Him.
2. He created it, and He is the owner of it.
3. Everything in this world counts.

As Christians, we believe that everything in this world is going to be accounted for.

What does "everything" mean? Not just the big things like your home, cars, or investments, but paying the bills, balancing your checkbook, and maintaining your house and yard.

Remember, a steward is a manager of another's property, finances, or other affairs. For us to be wise with what God has entrusted to us, we need to be effective managers for God.

THE EFFECTIVE MONEY MANAGER

If you assume the job of Effective Money Manager for your family, your job description will center around three different areas of responsibility. The key word here is "responsible."

A money manager must take inventory, be responsible with the things he's been entrusted with, and steer a clear course through investments. Let's look at how we are to function within each of these three areas.

1. Take responsibility for all your possessions.

Everything you own needs to be taken care of — from the car to the kids' bicycles; from the house to the tool shed.

If your house has a deck — or anything built with treated lumber — you know the meaning of "care"; it's spelled w-o-r-k.

Each year, *every* board in the deck — from floor to steps to railings — must be scrubbed with a toxic compound to eliminate mold and mildew, then hosed down, and sealed with a protective coating.

When Ken built his house 12 years ago, he didn't realize that this process needed to be done every summer. As a result, the wood on his deck rotted. To make matters worse, the green slime from the mildew seeped through the boards to the cement patio below, permanently staining it.

Last summer Ken had a new deck installed. (We won't talk about what that cost!)

"This year I'm going to clean the deck for sure!" he told his wife. "To make it easier, I think I'll rent one of those power washers."

"Be careful," his wife told him. "I read those things are really powerful!"

"Not to worry," he said smugly — in typical Ken "the toolman" style.

When his wife returned from shopping, she noticed her husband sweeping the deck.

"What are all those little pieces of wood?" she asked.

"The top layer of the deck," he mumbled without looking up.

Aside from maintaining your possessions, you also have to keep track of them.

If you permit a friend to borrow a tool or a vehicle — or even a road map — you want the item returned in the same condition you loaned it.

I know a guy who won't learn his lesson. Four times he's loaned his copy of *The Rise and Fall of the Third Reich;* and four times the loan-ee has failed to return it. This has been going on since 1966! Something is wrong with that picture.

2. Be responsible to God for all your purchases.

Everything I buy is purchased with God's money — which He has entrusted to me. Just as a money manager is responsible to his investors, we are responsible to make wise decisions with God's money.

Women may be impulsive when it comes to buying, but men have another flaw. Their motto is: "Let's just get this over with." Or, "Don't sweat the small stuff." Operating in that mode can result in poor decision-making and greater expense in the long run.

When Jim and Pam built their first house, every detail had to be carefully thought through. With both of them working full-time jobs, time was already a precious commodity. Months of making selections and the endless decisions about the house wore them down.

"The contractor says we have to hire our own painters," Pam told her husband one evening.

"Go ahead, just keep me out of it!" he responded with a wave of his hand.

With no time to check references, Pam turned to the yellow pages and called an advertised painter, who came out and gave her an estimate. She selected the colors, and he started to work.

When he showed Pam the final bill, she nearly had a heart attack. "This is nearly twice the price you quoted me!"

"The price I quoted was for the labor. That didn't include the paint," he stated. "I thought you knew that."

In this case, Jim's "hands-off" attitude cost him a bundle.

3. You are responsible for the outcome.

Ron Blue says, "You can't fake stewardship." In other words, your priorities in life are revealed in your checkbook.[1]

If you were to allow me to review your checkbook register, I could tell fairly accurately what is important to you.

Is *how* we spend our money significant? Absolutely, because we are going to be held accountable for our actions and decisions.

Jesus shared a parable about a nobleman who entrusted his money to his employees before leaving on a business trip. When he returned, he expected to collect his money, including any interest earned. He gave one man $5,000, another $2,000, and the last $1,000. (See Matt. 25:14-30.)

The $5K and $2K guys immediately put their money to work in an effort to make interest off of their investments. The $1K guy, however, buried his money in a hole in his backyard because he was afraid of losing it.

When the master returned, he asked for his money back. The $5K and $2K men had both doubled their money, returning $10,000 and $4,000 respectively to their master.

How did the nobleman respond? With equal commendations of praise for both stewards. To the first he said, " 'You have been faithful in handling this small amount,' he told him, 'so now I will give you many more responsibilities. Begin the joyous tasks I have assigned to you' " (Matt. 25:21). And to the second: " 'Good work,' his master said. 'You are a good and faithful servant. You have been faithful over this small amount, so now I will give you much more' " (Matt. 25:23).

To the man with $1,000, however, the master had this rebuke: "Wicked man! Lazy slave! Since you knew I would demand your profit, you should at least have put my money into the bank so I could have some interest. Take the money from this man and give it to the man with the $10,000. For the man who uses well what he is given shall be given more, and he shall have abundance. But from the man who is unfaithful, even what little responsibility he has shall be taken from him" (Matt. 25:26-29).

Don't be like the man with $1K who was ousted because of his laziness and ineffective use of the money his master had entrusted to him.

The amount of money you have does not matter to God. Like the nobleman, God is pleased as long as you use the amount you are given wisely.

Are you doing the very best you can with your money?

Principles That Can Make or Break You

OWE GOD WHAT IS HIS

In an age when many people don't even acknowledge the existence of God, it might seem strange to say that we all "owe Him." But owe we do, and we are commanded to tithe a tenth of our income back to God's work. Jesus said that we are to pay Caesar what is Caesar's, but also to pay God what is His.

After the people of Israel returned to their homeland from captivity in Babylon, the prophets Nehemiah and Ezra had established ritual and political reforms. Spiritually, however, the people were bankrupt — in more ways than one.

Through the prophet Malachi, God confronts His people with the truth: "Will a man rob God? Surely not! And yet you have robbed me" (Mal. 3:8).

In spite of their miraculous deliverance from slavery and bondage, the people of Israel refused to let go of what mattered most to them — money. They were hoarding the tenth of their income that rightfully belonged to their Deliverer. Worst of all, they didn't think they had done anything wrong.

"How?" they asked

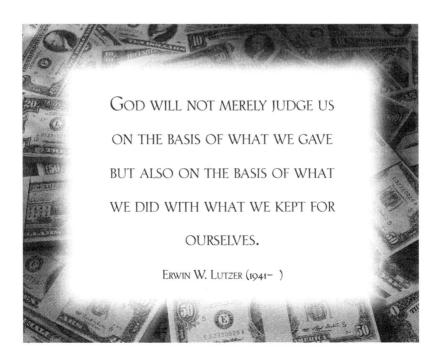

GOD WILL NOT MERELY JUDGE US

ON THE BASIS OF WHAT WE GAVE

BUT ALSO ON THE BASIS OF WHAT

WE DID WITH WHAT WE KEPT FOR

OURSELVES.

ERWIN W. LUTZER (1941–)

"You have robbed me of the tithes and offerings due to me" (vs. 9).

Then God gives them a command followed by a wonderful promise: "Bring all the tithes into the storehouse so that there will be food enough in my Temple; if you do, I will open up the windows of heaven for you and pour out a blessing so great you won't have room enough to take it in!"

Wow!

"Try it!" God suggests. "Let me prove it to you!" (Mal. 3:10) He then outlines the payback for their obedience:

- "Your crops will be large, for I will guard them from insects and plagues" (vs. 11). (Your business/income won't be eaten away by debt.)
- "Your grapes won't shrivel away before they ripen" (vs. 11). (Your investments won't go under before they come to maturity.)
- "All nations will call you blessed" (vs. 12). (Everyone will know God has blessed you.)
- "You will be a land sparkling with happiness" (vs. 12). (You'll know true joy and fulfillment in life.)

Great! Sign me up! you say.

Don't forget the tithe is 10 percent of your income — the amount shown on your pay stub *before* all the deductions are taken out. Still interested?

Why does God require that we pay our tithes and offerings? Surely he doesn't need our money to run the universe!

It's not that *He* needs our money; it's that *we* need to give it — as an act of love and obedience. That's why He tests our submission to Him as our King at the place dearest to our heart — the pocketbook! Money is the "acid test" of our love and commitment to God.

PRINCIPLES OF GIVING

Like most Christians, I read my Bible, pray, and attend church, but true fulfillment in Christ did not come until I learned how to give. Why? Because I know with every gift I give, I am allowing Christ to mold me to become more like Him. When we give to further God's kingdom here on earth, we open the way for Him to bless us in a way only He can.

Many believers misunderstand the principle of giving. In fact, people ask me more questions about "giving" than any other subject. Yet, the second most important subject in the Bible — besides salvation — is the principle of giving.

Let's look at the principles of giving so you can understand the purpose of it and gain abundant life with Christ.

1. Before you eat, plant a seed.

The apostle Paul wrote: "But remember this — if you give little, you will get little. A farmer who plants just a few seeds will get only a small crop, but if he plants much, he will reap much" (2 Cor. 9:6).

If a farmer only takes a handful of seeds and throws them over the ground, he will get a handful of food to eat. But if a farmer takes a bag full of seeds and scatters them on the ground, he will receive a bag full of food to eat. This is the old principle of sowing and reaping.

Sometimes it does not make sense to give. In Isaiah 55:8, God says, "My ways are not your ways."

Unexpected hospital bills may have left you in debt, and every month you get further behind. Should you be expected to give? Yes. When you have a need, plant a seed. The man who planted all his seeds had a bigger crop at harvest time.

What are some of the ways people try to solve financial problems? Beg, borrow, steal, win the lottery, work longer hours, or get another job.

What is God's way to solve our financial problems? Give.

Jesus said, "Give, and it will be given to you. A good measure, pressed down, shaken together and running over, will be poured into your lap. For with the measure you use, it will be measured to you" (Luke 6:38;NIV).

2. God will supply all your "needs" not your "wants"?

We should never give to get something back in return so we can fulfill all our desires. "My God will meet all your needs according to his glorious riches in Christ Jesus" (Phil. 4:19;NIV). Keep in mind that this verse says: "all your needs," not "all your wants."

What's the difference between a "want" and a "need"? A "want" is something you desire, but you really don't need. A "need" is something that keeps your life in harmony with God's will.

For example, a "want" would be a brand new dining room table in the latest style from the *Country Home* magazine. "A need" would be a large table and enough chairs so you can eat together comfortably as a family.

One family needed a second vehicle after their old car "gave up the ghost." Trying to get by using only one car proved difficult since Dad had to drive it to work, Mom needed a way to run errands, and their teenage son had to be transported to and from basketball practice.

"Lord, we really need another vehicle, please provide one for us," they prayed day after day.

While Dad envisioned a four-wheel drive Jeep, Mom saw herself driving a new, red Buick, and Johnny dreamed about a black Mustang. All three were focused on what they "wanted" rather than on what they "needed." As a result, their prayers went unanswered.

After months of juggling times and schedules around the one car, reality set it. A family discussion brought them to the conclusion that their budget could only afford a small used car with low mileage and in good condition. They began to pray specifically for the kind of car they "needed."

Not long after they came to this agreement, Johnny mentioned to a mechanic friend that his family was looking for a used car.

"Really?" the mechanic asked. "My neighbor's husband just died, and she wants to sell their car since she can't drive. I can check it out for you, and call you with a price."

Within a week the family bought the car, which had low mileage, was in excellent condition, and only a few years old — all at half the going rate! It wasn't a Jeep or a Buick or a Mustang, but it was exactly what they needed!

Remember, "all your needs" will be met.

3. Give with an attitude of love.

What kind of attitude does God require? An attitude of love.

"If I give all my possessions to feed the poor . . . but do not have *love,* it profits me nothing" (1 Cor. 13:3;NAS).

God set the example for us: "For God so *loved* the world, that

MONEY IS A GOOD SERVANT, BUT A DANGEROUS MASTER.

DOMINIQUE BOUHOURS (1628–1702)

He gave His only begotten Son, that whoever believes in Him shall not perish, but have eternal life" (John 3:16;NAS).

Without love the gift has no true value. God loved us so much that He gave his Son to die for our sins, so that we may live forever.

Our giving should be a love offering to the Lord — not to the church, ministries, or individuals.

GIVING WITH THE RIGHT ATTITUDE

How can we make sure we are giving with an attitude of love? The apostle Paul laid out the conditions in this verse: "Each one must do just as he has purposed in his heart: not grudgingly or under compulsion for God loves a cheerful giver" (2 Cor. 9:7;NAS).

Let's look at the principles God wants to teach us.

1. Think through your giving.

What does "purposed in his heart" mean?

God wants you to plan your giving and put some thought into how much you are going to give. In addition, you need to know the character and objectives of the person or ministry to whom you plan to contribute.

2. Be enthusiastic about giving.

God wants you to be excited to be giving to Him — "not grudgingly."

When the offering plate is passed at church, do you turn to your spouse with a look that says, "Here goes some of my hard-earned money"? If so, you are a grudging giver.

If you want to receive God's blessings in return, be excited that you are contributing to the kingdom of God.

3. Give because you want to.

If you feel guilty and give because you think you are obligated, you are giving "under compulsion." With that kind of attitude, you won't get any credit for it.

God wants you to give because you are thankful for what He has done in your past and what He will do in the future.

4. Give cheerfully.

The root word for miserable is "miser."

God loves a person who loves to give. "God loves a cheerful giver." The happiest people I know give the most to God's kingdom.

My father-in-law always refers to this principle about giving — and puts it into practice as well. This is the secret to becoming a cheerful giver.

THREE THINGS TO REMEMBER

Always remember to keep a mental picture of the Source of your possessions. In the seat next to you, watching and caring, is God.

1. Remember Who is the source of all money.

"For God, who gives seed to the farmer to plant, and later on, good crops to harvest and eat, will give you more and more seed to plant and will make it grow so that you can give away more and more fruit from your harvest" (2 Cor. 9:10).

Since God owns everything, He is the one "who gives seed." God supplies us with all of our resources and the talent to make money.

I often remind myself that 100 percent of my money is God's money, and I am thankful He lets me live on 90 percent of it. The other 10 percent belongs to Him, and if I keep it for myself I will be robbing God.

We give to show God that He is the center of our world and that we are thankful for what He has done in our past. Giving also releases our faith to believe that He will provide for us in the future.

2. Remember: God does not need your money.

He owns "the cattle on a thousand hills" (Ps. 50:10) and lives in a city where "the great street . . . was of pure gold" (Rev. 21:21;NIV).

If you were as rich as Microsoft's Bill Gates — who is worth $51 billion — and you decided to give half your money to God, what would God's response be? Would He be impressed and say, "Oh, thank you! Thank you! I really needed that money to run my universe!"? I don't think so.

Why then does God's Word repeatedly teach us to give? We should give for two reasons: (1) God commands us to; (2) to further the work of God's kingdom on this earth.

If God so desired, He could rain money from heaven to pay the salaries of every pastor and missionary in the world. He doesn't. Why not? Because He wants to use our money — and our giving of it — to test our hearts. Giving is the secret to finding fulfillment.

God always looks at the heart — not the amount — of the giver. Jesus said, concerning the poor widow who gave a measly two pennies into the offering, "He called his disciples to him and remarked, 'That poor widow has given more than all those rich men put together! For they gave a little of their extra fat, while she gave up her last penny' " (Mark 12:43-44).

Principles That Can Make or Break You

3. Remember God's commitment.

"Yes, God will give you much so that you can give away much, and when we take your gifts to those who need them they will break out into thanksgiving and praise to God for your help" (2 Cor. 9:11).

A boy growing up in England in the 1800s saw his father, an Anglican priest, dragged off to debtor's prison. Although the son was oppressed by poverty all through his childhood and never saw his father get out of debt, the boy chose to follow in his father's vocation.

Instead of becoming a priest, John became a professor at Oxford University, earning 30 pounds a year — which was more than enough for a single man to live comfortably. For the first time in his life, John had enough money to pursue the pleasures that only wealth could bring. He spent his money playing cards, buying tobacco, and brandy.

One winter day, when a chambermaid came to his door, John noticed that she was wearing only a thin linen gown. Realizing that this lady must be freezing in the cold, he reached into his pocket and found nothing. John then wondered, *Would my Master say, "Well done, good and faithful servant" — or something else?*

John decided to calculate his living expenses and devise a budget for himself. He found that 28 pounds a year would meet all his needs. That left him 2 pounds to give away.

Although his income doubled the next year, John still lived on 28 pounds and was able to give away 32 pounds. When his income increased to 90 pounds, he continued to live on 28 pounds, giving away 62 pounds. Another raise brought him to 120 pounds. Still, the same 28 pounds went toward living expenses, and 92 pounds was given to help others.

Who was this man? John Wesley, who believed that "with increasing income, the Christian standard of giving should increase, not his standard of living."

As the founder of the Methodist Church in England and America, and a prolific writer, John Wesley eventually earned close to 1,400 pounds a year. Although he became one of the wealthiest men in England, Wesley continued to live off of 28 pounds and give away the rest. This means he donated 1,372 pounds a year to helping others, which is the equivalent of over a million dollars today!

Throughout his life, John Wesley continued to be associated with the poor and even lived among them in homes that his

WHEN I HAVE MONEY, I GET RID OF
IT AS QUICKLY AS POSSIBLE, LEST IT
FIND A WAY INTO MY HEART.

JOHN WESLEY (1703–1791)

· ·

contributions helped build in London. When Wesley died in 1791, the only money he owned was the coins left in his pocket.

More concerned about the Master's opinion of him as a good steward than about having a good time, John Wesley did not seek to please man or to impress God with his giving. He simply chose to be a good manger of the resources God had entrusted to him. At the same time, God was faithful to His promises and continued to bless John Wesley financially throughout his lifetime.

BENEFITS OF GIVING

Planned, cheerful, and enthusiastic giving brings with it many blessings. What are the benefits of giving? God's Word suggests at least four:

1. Strengthens our relationship with Christ.
"For where your treasure is, there your heart will be also" (Matt. 6:21;NIV).

2. Makes us more Christ-like.
After all, the ultimate giver in life is God. "He gave His only begotten son" (John 3:16;NAS).

3. Shapes us.
"Instruct them . . . to be generous and ready to share . . . so that they may take hold of that which is life indeed" (1 Tim. 6:18-19;NAS).

4. Provides great returns.
"But store up for yourselves treasures in heaven,

where moth nor rust do not destroy, and thieves do not break in or steal" (Matt. 6:20;NIV).

THE DISTRACTION OF POSSESSIONS

God knew that money was going to be a major distraction to our walk with Him. That's why Jesus warned us: "The attractions of this world and the delights of wealth, and the search for success and the lure of nice things come in and crowd out God's message" (Mark 4:19).

I could name many nice things I would love to have — like better golf clubs, a new truck, a high-powered computer — and the list could go on. My wife always accuses me of having a bigger Christmas list than the kids!

The ongoing accumulation of possessions distracts more young married couples from God's purpose for their lives than any other temptation. Jesus warned against this powerful diversion when He said: "No servant can serve two masters. Either he will hate the one and love the other, or he will be devoted to the one and despise the other. You cannot serve God and Money" (Luke 16:13;NIV).

For years, Steve worked in construction, barely making enough to provide for his family. Tired of the constant financial pressure, he decided — at age 32 — to go back to school to become an x-ray technician. After graduating at the top of his class, he was offered several lucrative positions in area hospitals. He accepted one and began his new job.

"I don't know," Steve said one day to his wife. "I'm not sure this is what God wants me to do with my life."

"Really?" Julie asked. "But you're doing so well. I thought you enjoyed it."

"I do, but God keeps speaking to me about working with kids and teens." For several years, Steve and Julie had taken short-term mission trips to Mexico City where they ministered to street kids using mime, drama, and puppets.

"And just when I was getting used to having money left over at the end of the month!" Julie joked, and then suggested, "Let's pray about it." Not distracted by worldly pursuits and the lure of "living the American dream," their hearts and ears were tuned to receive God's guidance.

Steve and Julie decided to candidate for the job of youth pastor at a local church. They also began researching mission organizations who needed their specific gifts and talents.

The same day they were offered the youth pastor job, a letter came from a mission group in Mexico asking them to join their staff.

Within a few months, Steve and Julie had raised their support money, packed up their belongings and their two kids, and were on their way south of the border.

Does Steve regret giving up a good salary and a promising career to serve among the poor and lost in a Third World country? "Absolutely not," he says. "After all, I'm laying up my treasure in heaven!"

IS MONEY EVIL?

Many Christians consider money evil and the accumulation of wealth a wicked pursuit.

Is money evil? Before answering fully, let me ask you this rhetorical question: Is food evil?

Let's get real. Both money and food are necessary for existence on this planet. We need both in order to survive. It's not how much money or food we have, but how we use our resources.

Does the Bible say that money is "the root of all evil"? No. Here's the actual quote from 1 Timothy 6:10: "For the love of money is a root of all kinds of evil." It is the *love* of money that is evil.

Wall Street, a popular movie from several years ago, highlights the problem that the love of money creates. The main character, Gordon Gekko declared that "Greed is good." This became the film's signature line, but what does it say about our society?

Compared to the living standards of the rest of the world, most Americans are rich. The wealth we enjoy in this country has come, not because we are more ingenious or "lucky" than other peoples of the world, but because God in His mercy has blessed our nation.

I've heard it said that the average American has access to more "stuff" than kings did 100 years ago. We live in a nation of luxury.

As Christians we need not be ashamed to have money, but we are expected to constantly remind ourselves of the source of our prosperity, as the apostle Paul told Pastor Timothy:

> Tell those who are rich not to be proud and not to trust in their money, which will soon be gone, but their pride and trust should be in the living God who always richly gives us all we need for our enjoyment. Tell them to use their money to do good. They should be rich in

good works and should give happily to those in need, always being ready to share with others whatever God has given them (1 Tim. 6:17-18).

Notice that Paul instructs Timothy not to tell the rich to give up all their money, quit their jobs, or share equally with others. Instead, he has this message for the rich: Don't forget who gave you your riches and keep focusing on God as your hope — and not on money.

The rich young man we discussed earlier refused to give up his wealth when Jesus asked him to sell it all and give it to the poor and follow Him. Instead, the man's love of money and possessions distracted him from the most precious blessing of all — eternal life.

You can avoid the money trap by acknowledging that God owns 100 percent of everything you have and by giving God what is rightfully His. If you do, you will live a happy life.

God says, He will "pour out a blessing so great you won't have room enough to take it in!" (Mal. 3:10). Your life will be filled with more contentment than you have ever known.

As you get your financial house in order, you may find yourself asking, "What should I do with this extra income?"

The next chapter outlines how to make more without working harder. If you follow the prescribed steps, you can become a wise investor without developing a Wall Street ulcer!

CHAPTER ELEVEN

INVESTING – IT'S
NEVER TOO LATE

WHAT DO you think is the number one concern among couples regarding the future? You probably guessed it: Will we have enough money to retire without sacrificing our current lifestyle?

If you are worried about your retirement, when should you start preparing for the future? NOW! It is never too early nor too late to start investing.

The check you'll receive from Social Security when you reach retirement will average well below $700 a month. Even today many American retirees are unable to maintain the lifestyle level they once enjoyed. They have gone from upper middle-class to poverty because they thought Social Security would take care of them.

A few years ago an elderly couple living in Phoenix died during record-setting summer heat because they could not afford an air-conditioner in their home.

Researchers estimate that by the year 2010, the increasing number of retirees in America will create problems for Social Security. At that point the nation's number of tax-paying citizens will be too small to support the number of people qualified for Social Security benefits.

With that in mind, I suggest you consider Social Security — not as future income — but merely as a "possible" added bonus. That puts the ball in your court. It's up to you to plan and prepare for your own retirement needs.

The earlier you start investing, the less you will have to put aside overall. What's the difference between planning early and planning late? The amount of money you will need to reach your desired retirement goal.

The earlier you begin investing in a retirement 401K or IRA, the sooner compound interest will begin to work for you.

In the chapter on debt, I showed how interest rates work *against* you. In this chapter, we will have an opportunity to see how interest rates work *for* you.

MEET THE EXTRAVAGANTS AND THE ORDINARYS

Meet my favorite two couples — John and Betty Extravagant and Bob and Sally Ordinary. Let's follow them through the first five years of married life.

After graduating from college, the two couples get married around the same time. The newlywed husbands, John and Bob, find employment at a computer company, and Betty and Sally get jobs at a clothing store. Both couples make exactly the same amount of money each month — $1,000.

The Extravagants decide to rent a condo for $450 a month (with utilities included) in the nicer part of town. The Ordinarys choose to rent an apartment for $250 a month (with utilities included) in a working-class section of the city.

As soon as the Extravagants are settled, they make their first purchase.

"I really like the new Mustang that came out this year," John tells Betty.

"Me, too," she agrees. "Let's buy it! We can use my parents' $2,000 wedding present as a down payment."

"Great idea," John responds. "The car costs $20,000, so we can finance the remaining $18,000. The dealer says it will only take five years at 11 percent interest."

Across town, the Ordinarys are also preparing to purchase a car with a wedding gift of $2,000 from their parents.

"I found a great deal on a used Honda Accord," Bob informs Sally. "If we use the money from our wedding gifts, we can buy it and won't have to make car payments."

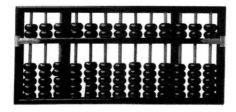

RICHES SERVE A WISE
MAN BUT COMMAND
A FOOL.

ENGLISH PROVERB

"Sounds good to me," Sally agrees.

On payday, the Extravagants deposit their combined income of $1,000 and go to a fancy restaurant to celebrate. The next day, however, their monthly bills arrive.

"With our monthly rent of $450 and the $400 car payment, we barely have anything to live on," Betty whines.

"Stop worrying," John insists. "The guys at work are really impressed with our new Mustang. And it sure looks nice in our driveway."

Meanwhile, out of their $1,000 paycheck, the Ordinarys are paying $250 on rent, investing $400 in a mutual fund, and living on the rest.

A few months later, the Extravagants are having regrets about their no-longer new car.

"If you hadn't gotten that ding on the door," Betty points out to John, "the Mustang would still look good."

"What a bummer," John grumbles. "Nobody seems to notice the car anymore."

The Ordinarys continue to put away $400 a month while the Extravagances are making $400 a month car payments on a quickly depreciating vehicle.

Let's fast-forward to five years down the road.

The Extravagants are making their final $400 payment on their Mustang, having paid a total of $26,000 for a car that cost $20,000 new. Now, five years later, the car is worth $5,000.

During that same time, the Ordinarys were faithfully putting away $400 a month into a mutual fund that has grown to $30,000 in value.

"I called a real estate agent today," Sally tells Bob.

"Great!" Bob responds. "With the amount we've saved, we can start looking for a house in the nicer sections of town."

THE TRUTH ABOUT INVESTING

Investing is not about being smart enough to pick the right stock at the right time. Investing is a tool we can use to be good stewards with the surplus God has given us.

In addition to tithing, investing is your surest route to financial security.

The Extravagants started married life in debt by buying a car they could not afford. Not only did it cost them more money than the car was worth, but they immediately put a tremendous burden on their budget. With only $150 a month left for other expenses, how did they manage?

Perhaps the Extravagants lived off their credit cards during those first five years. If so, it would probably take them the next 10 years to pay off all their debts — even if they stopped using their credit cards.

By living in the nicer part of town and purchasing a new car, the Extravagants appeared to be prosperous in the beginning. The Ordinarys, however, seemed to be barely making ends meet. They lived in an average part of town and owned a used car that already had dings.

Unlike the Extravagants who were paying money to borrow, the Ordinarys were putting money away for the future and making interest on their money. Although $400 a month may not seem like a lot at first, after time the money begins to grow.

And that's the key word — *time*. Time is your friend when you are investing and saving. "But he who gathers money little by little makes it grow" (Prov. 13:11;NIV). Time is your friend — not your enemy.

Many young couples live under the illusion, "We've got to have it now!" The idea of saving money to buy the things we want is a foreign thought to most young Americans. In fact, saving is not even an option — especially if we "want it now"!

"I'll just charge it!" And what do you get? Instant gratification. Or, at least, "temporary" gratification until the credit card bill arrives in the mail.

Reacting quickly and going into debt to satisfy every whim can result in bankruptcy. "Steady plodding brings prosperity; hasty speculation brings poverty" (Prov. 21:5). Time is our friend, and steady saving brings prosperity.

Until the late 1960s, Americans were a saving people. Today, however, Americans save an average of only 4 percent of their income. Other countries such as Japan, India, Germany, Taiwan, and China save up to 10-20 percent of their income.

For nearly 40 years Americans have been bombarded with TV advertising trying to sell us everything from shaving cream to satellite dishes. At some point we need to grow up and get a life!

Our yearnings will always be greater than our earnings — unless we're Donald Trump or Bill Gates. And, even they have limits!

INVESTING – IT'S NEVER TOO LATE

Every day I see things I would love to have — and some of it I could actually use! After all, who doesn't want — and need — a 20 horsepower riding mower or $80-an-ounce perfume? After all, "I'm worth it!" At least, that's what the TV commercials tell me.

In the beginning of this book, I shared how I impulsively went into debt to buy a new truck that Kari and I could not afford. Fortunately, I quickly realized I was mortgaging our future with that unwise purchase.

"I'm going to take the truck back," I told Kari. "Maybe I can get an older, four-door sedan that we can afford." Facing that car dealer was "life's most embarrassing moment" for me, but it was a lesson I will never forget.

Starting that day, I saved and eventually was able to pay cash for the new car I wanted.

STEPS TO BECOMING AN INVESTOR

When you see the words "saving and investing," what comes to mind? Big-ticket items like a new house, your kid's college education, or retirement? How about saving money for smaller, short-term projects like taking your dream vacation, buying a new computer, or giving more to your favorite missionaries?

The first step toward saving money is a giant step for many people. Believe it or not, you *can* enjoy financial freedom and still have the things you need and want — if you follow these steps:

1. Eliminate unnecessary debt.

The first step to an effective saving program is to eliminate unnecessary debt. This usually does not include your home mortgage — unless you got in over your head, and the monthly payment is beyond your means. In that case, you may need to sell your house and purchase one you can afford.

Credit cards, car loans, student loans, etc. that charge anywhere from 8 to 21 percent interest must go! Show no mercy. Get tough and start hacking away. Using the debt reduction plan outlined in chapter 9, you can eventually save yourself hundreds — if not thousands — of dollars in the long run.

Paying off your debts is the first phase of investing. Once all your debts — outside of your home mortgage — are paid off, you are on your way to becoming an investor.

2. Take a pro-active role in managing your finances.

I hear countless stories of people who have worked hard to earn their money, and yet lost it. Why? Because someone in a suit sitting behind a desk told them, "If you let me manage your money, here's what I'll do for you."

Financial planners, stock brokers, and other helpful professionals do indeed help people make wise decisions with their money. Unfortunately, there are plenty of money-hungry "sharks" looking for easy prey.

Before you get involved in investing, do your own research and read as many investment books as possible. *Learn to Earn* by Peter Lynch provides many practical and useful tips for the new investor.

The best investors are those who take a pro-active role in managing their finances.

3. Build an emergency account.

Start by saving an amount equal to three-to-six months of your income and put it in a money market account. This account will serve as your emergency account to be used in case any unfortunate circumstances arise.

In the past you have been forced to charge emergency expenses on a credit card. Now instead of mortgaging the future, you can borrow from yourself — and instead of paying interest, you'll be making interest.

4. Build a savings fund for short-term needs.

In chapter 8, you and your spouse learned how to set goals and develop a spending plan. You may have listed several short-term needs like a new car, furniture, Christmas gifts, and a summer vacation.

Now comes the hard part: Saving the money to make your goals and dreams come to pass.

First, decide how much money you are going to set aside each month, and begin putting that amount into a money market account.

5. Build a long-term saving fund.

In your planning session, you and your spouse probably listed some fairly expensive items that you would like to acquire in the future. Saving for these dreams needs to be put into a conservative interest-bearing account like a growth-oriented mutual fund.

If you are like me, you do not have time to read *The Wall Street Journal* every day or keep up on the latest development in stocks or analyze companies' annual reports. That's why I like mutual funds.

A mutual fund is a group of people who pool their money together and let professional, experienced investors separate the bad from the good companies. By analyzing hundreds of reports, a mutual fund coordinator tries to find companies with the potential to become the next McDonalds, Gap, or Nike.

TEN REASONS TO INVEST IN MUTUAL FUNDS

Here are ten reasons why mutual funds work well for new investors:

1. Makes you a player.

Mutual funds allow the average person to invest with different companies. It takes lots of money to buy into a company — not counting the commission fees involved in the transaction.

2. Easy to get started.

As soon as you sign a one-page form and give the mutual fund directors your money, you instantly become an owner of 25 to 200 different companies. If you agree to a monthly automatic deposit into your mutual fund account, you can begin with as little as $25 to $50 a month.

3. You can add money at anytime.

You sign up for the automatic deposit or contribute quarterly, semi-annually, or annually. *When* you put money in does not matter.

GOD HAS CHARGED HIMSELF WITH FULL RESPONSIBILITY FOR OUR ETERNAL HAPPINESS AND STANDS READY TO TAKE OVER THE MANAGEMENT OF OUR LIVES.

A.W. TOZER (1897–1963)

4. Reduces risk through diversification.

Instead of depending on one company to make a profit, you will be invested in as many as 200 different companies. One company may have a bad year, while another company could be experiencing record profits.

5. Reduces your anxiety level.

Having your hard-earned money invested with different

companies and industries eliminates worrying about a certain company or industry having a down year.

6. No-load funds have no commission fees.

Loaded funds have a commission that is passed on to the investor. The fee can be as much as 5 – 8.5 percent on every dollar you invest.

For example, if you invest $100 in a load fund, $5 will go to the stockbroker/salesman who sells you the fund. A no-load fund skips the sales force, advertises their fund, and provides an 800 number for you to call to get started. By skipping the sales force, you save $5, and you get the full $100 working for you.

7. A full-time professional works for you.

Your fund manager spends 100 percent of his time making the fund successful. In fact, the manager's pay is usually tied to the performance of the fund.

8. Past performance is public information.

A printed "prospectus" provides important information on the history and performance of the mutual fund. You can know before you invest how the fund has performed in the past.

9. You can redeem part or all of your shares with a single phone call.

If you need to get your money — for whatever reason — you can call them and tell them how much you want to take out.

10. The Security and Exchange Commission closely regulates mutual funds.

Since mutual fund companies deal with millions and billions of dollars, they are watched closely by the investor's policeman. If anything suspicious happens, the S.E.C. is on top of it.

YOUR FRIEND – TIME

You may be wondering, "Isn't investing in the stock exchange risky business? How will I know when to pull out my money, so I don't lose everything?"

Market timing is very hard to do. If someone developed a system of timing the market just perfect he/she would pass Bill Gates as the world's richest person.

If you were to time the market perfectly and bought at the absolute highest moment each successive year since 1970, your annual return would be 8.5 percent. If you bought at the lowest point, your annual return would be 10.1 percent. The difference between a good and bad timer is just 1.6 percent, which is not much of a difference.

Stay in for the long term, and don't expect to make money quickly off the market. Remember, time is your friend.

Investing provides security for the future — although nothing is absolute in this world.

Time has proven, however, that putting away a small amount of money in an average investment over an extended period of time produces good rewards. You may not get rich, but it would be enough for a husband and wife to spoil their grandchildren and take that European vacation you've been planning for years.

Investing may be a great vehicle to prosperity, but it is not our greatest commodity. In the next chapter, you will find that our most valuable commodity is something we all have but often fail to recognize.

CHAPTER TWELVE
IN SEARCH OF OUR
GREATEST COMMODITY

FRANK and Judy married the summer following college graduation.

After returning from their honeymoon, Frank immediately started his new job with a software company. Judy taught second grade.

Both left for work every morning around 7:00 a.m. Judy got home by 4:00 p.m. and Frank arrived at 5:30 p.m.

After three months of marriage, Judy began to notice that Frank was putting in longer hours at the office. Slowly he had extended his work schedule, often arriving home after 9:00 p.m.

"I can't understand why you are getting home so late," Judy often mentioned to Frank.

"I'm working on a very important project that needs to be finished soon," Frank told her.

Judy took Frank's explanation to mean that his boss had given him this assignment.

Soon after the project was completed, Judy noticed that Frank's schedule had not changed. In fact, some days Frank put in even longer hours. Again, Judy thought that Frank was complying with the company's expectations.

Then one day, Frank told Judy, "I've decided to join a toastmasters group that meets every Thursday night at seven."

"Really?" Judy asked, stunned that Frank had time for his Thursday night meetings, but was not able to come home sooner.

Time passed and, during the summer, Judy announced, "I'm pregnant!"

Both she and Frank were thrilled.

"I don't think I'll go back to teaching in the fall," Judy told Frank.

Surely, a baby will bring Frank home, she thought.

After the baby was born, however, nothing changed. Frank continued to put in long hours, attend his Thursday night toastmasters meetings and even joined the city basketball league.

"How can you make time to play basketball, but you can't come home sooner?" Judy exploded to Frank one day.

Kari and I knew Frank and Judy from church. In fact, Frank and I were good friends, and I had noticed that his schedule seemed to be out of balance.

"We're starting a small group Bible study for newlyweds," I told Frank. "Why don't you and Judy come?"

I knew Judy was hurting desperately because her husband had been more focused on other things than on her.

"The longest marriage in the group is two years, and the shortest just returned from their honeymoon," I told Frank, and he thought it was a great idea.

The first meeting started off with a bang.

Almost immediately, Judy attacked Frank.

"He never spends any time with me or the baby!" she complained. "In fact, I'm beginning to wonder what Frank is doing with his time!"

As the leader of the group, I tried to steer the conversation toward more positive topics.

Judy, however, had been so hurt by Frank that she saw this as her only opportunity to confront him about his neglect of their family.

THE GREATEST BENEFITS GOD HAS CONFERRED ON HUMAN LIFE, FATHERHOOD, MOTHERHOOD, CHILDHOOD, HOME, BECOME THE GREATEST CURSE IF JESUS CHRIST IS NOT THE HEAD.

OSWALD CHAMBERS
(1874–1917)

IN SEARCH OF OUR GREATEST COMMODITY

After the group had left, Kari said, "Why don't you call Frank and meet with him for lunch?"

"Yeah," I replied, "I know he was embarrassed about the whole thing. I hope they don't stop coming. I think Judy and Frank could use the support of a small group."

Then next day, I met Frank for lunch.

"I have never been so embarrassed in my whole life," he said as tears welled up in his eyes. "How could Judy attack me in front of our friends?"

"What's going on?" I asked, hoping to get Frank's side of the story.

"When Judy and I got engaged, we discussed our goals for the future. We planned to build our dream home within five years, own two nice cars, and be able to take exotic vocations."

"That's pretty ambitious," I said.

"I felt that I had to make our goals come true," Frank sighed, "or Judy wouldn't think that I was the man of her dreams."

I didn't know what to say.

"All I wanted was to provide a good living for my family," he continued. "The only reason I got involved in toastmasters and the basketball league was to do some networking. I thought if I knew the right people, I could get a promotion at work."

"What about all the long hours at work?" I asked.

"I needed the extra money," Frank explained. "When we first got married, we took on a lot of debt to buy nice furniture and new cars."

Frank was feeling the pressure of trying to make ends meet, and he did not want to disappoint Judy.

LIMITED TIME — UNLIMITED WISDOM

Time is our most valuable commodity. In fact, it is worth more than money, gold, silver, or anything else. The problem is: Our time is limited, and once it has been used, we cannot get it back.

All of us have the same number of minutes in an hour, hours in a day, days in a week, weeks in a month, and months in a year. No matter how hard you try, you cannot make more time.

Think of all the times you have entered into a project without consulting God first. I know I have done it hundreds of times.

Someone will say to me, "Hey, would like to help us put a building plan together for the new church?"

Without thinking twice I reply, "Sure!"

How easy it is to give an answer without praying first to get God's mind on the idea. "We should make plans — counting on God to direct us" (Prov. 16:9).

It is just plain dumb *not* to consult God first. After all, doesn't He know everything? "You saw me before I was born and scheduled each day of my life before I began to breathe" (Ps. 139:16). He is so all-knowing that even before you and I were born. He scheduled each day of our lives: ". . . which God prepared in advance for us to do" (Eph. 2:10;NIV). Usually, however, we think we know what is best.

Through prayer, His Word is our consultation. "Ask me and I will tell you some remarkable secrets about what is going to happen here" (Jer. 33:3). God is saying, "Just ask me!"

God is not suggesting that we do research and run tests to see what the situation may call for. All He wants us to do is to seek Him first.

His Word gives us tremendous insights. "I am but a pilgrim here on earth: how I need a map — and your commands are my chart and guide" (Ps. 119:19). God knows this earthly journey will have many forks in the road. That's why He has given us a map. The Bible points out safe routes to travel, the paths to avoid, and our final destination.

If you feel lost and don't know which road to take, consult God and He will direct your steps.

THE BIG TRADE-OFF

Most Americans believe they can make more time for themselves if they can get enough money.

Research indicates that Americans are the loneliest people in the world. We are also the hardest-working people in the world. Many of us believe that work is the answer to bringing us more time with our family.

"If I can just get this job promotion," the husband thinks, "I will be able to spend more time with my family." So he focuses on getting the job promotion and neglects the most important people in his life.

Like Frank, we think: If I can get the job promotion, it will mean more money, and then I won't need to worry about the bills. Unfortunately, how a spouse chooses to spend his or her time has caused many couples to divorce and families to split up.

IN SEARCH OF OUR GREATEST COMMODITY

"Our philosophy is not best expressed in words," Eleanor Roosevelt said. "It's expressed in choices one makes. In the long run, we shape our lives and we shape ourselves. The process never ends until the day we die. And the choices we make are ultimately our responsibility."

The choices we make are our responsibility. How we choose to spend our time is a decision that only you and I can make for ourselves. Yet, many people let the expectations of others dictate their schedule.

Frank let Judy and his work dictate his schedule. Even though he thought he was making his own decisions, Frank allowed outside influences to choose how he would spend his time.

A recent article in *The Wall Street Journal* highlights the need for priorities. Alan Robbins, who started his own company, Plastic Lumber, in 1989, discussed the pressures of being a business owner. One of the major topics in the interview centered on the time demands an owner faces.

Mr. Robbins stated, "The business had a role in the demise of the marriage." Ultimately, Mr. Robbins is getting a divorce, but he calls it "a trade-off he had to make . . . When you start a business like this, you have to deny your family a certain level of attention."

Later in the article he says he regrets not being able to spend more time with his kids. Somewhere along the path to success, this businessman forgot that his most important role is that of being a husband and father.[1]

The choices we make with our time have lasting impact. In order to obtain our goals, do we always have to sacrifice our family on the altar of success?

Well-known radio talk-show host and best-selling author Dr. Laura Schlessinger does not allow her job to control her life. Instead of sacrificing her family, she plans her schedule around the needs of her husband and son.

As a wife and mom, Dr. Schlessinger gets up at 5:00 a.m. — before anyone else — so she can work on her latest writing project. After her son is off to school, she prepares for her radio program.

She then goes to the station to host her show, "Dr. Laura," which is heard on over 430 radio stations. Nearly 18 million listeners tune in to get her opinion on their problems.

In spite of this high-pressure job, Dr. Schlessinger schedules her show so she can be home when her son returns from school. If she has any projects that need extra attention, she waits until her son and husband have turned in for the evening. Dr. Schlessinger maintains her success without sacrificing her family.[2]

PUTTING YOUR PRIORITIES IN ORDER

If you ask the typical American, "How are things going?" you will hear the reply, "Busy. I'm always on the go." Some make that statement with pride, while others groan as if carrying a heavy burden with no relief in sight.

Americans are programmed to be active. If we are not busy, then we think: I better get moving. I don't want people to think I'm lazy. The result: We let our activities dictate the way we prioritize our time.

Stephen Covey in his best-selling book, *Seven Habits of Highly Effective People,* says, "The key is not to prioritize your schedule, but to schedule your priorities."[3]

What is important to you? I have heard countless people say, "God is number one in my life!"

Yet if you ask a Christian about his quiet time or prayer time, he will often reply, "I am so busy. I have this major project due and have been working overtime; plus, I coach my daughter's softball team. I just can't find the time to read my Bible and pray." This person is activity-driven.

Instead of taking control of his life, he allows events and commitments to steer him where they want him to go. The result often leads to frustration and fatigue.

The key to gaining more time in your life is to prioritize and plan your days.

- Before you start making a list, consult
      God first.
- Next, review your priorities.
- Then, list your top five priorities.

How do you know what those are?

To help you out, let me propose a theoretical question. What if I were to tell you: I am going to take away everything you own or are connected to in this life — except for five things. What would those five things be?

Your list may consist of relationships, possessions, or maybe memories of the past. Take a few moments to think about your five most cherished things in life.

1.
2.
3.
4.
5.

How many of the five items are relationships? Did you list your spouse, children, family members, friends, or God?

Now think about your schedule for a typical day. Do the five important things you listed dictate your schedule? Are you activity-driven or relationship-driven?

Remember Mr. Robbins and Dr. Schlessinger? Mr. Robbins, the business owner, allowed his work to dictate his schedule. He divorced his family so he could attend to the affairs of running his business, which probably includes meetings, going over reports, attending to personnel matters, etc.

Dr. Schlessinger, on the other hand, lets her relationships dictate her schedule. She works when her family is asleep or away from home. In a magazine article titled, "Priorities," Dr. Schlessinger writes, "If my career in any way were interfering with the welfare of my child, I would turn in my resignation tomorrow. . . . I live for my family first, and my choices are based on that."[4]

Relationships have life-long significance; activities have temporary impact.

In his book, Stephen Covey writes about a father who was leaving the house with his children for a promised trip to the circus. When a phone call came for him to come to work, he declined. When his wife suggested that perhaps he should have gone to work, he responded, "The work will come again, but childhood won't."[5]

For the rest of their lives this man's children will remember this simple act. It served not only as an object lesson in priority-setting, but as an expression of their father's love.

A father who measures his priorities and chooses his children first will reap lifetime benefits. In fact, the positive effect will extend to future generations, as his children's children practice putting relationships before activities or work.

Some people, of course, are not in a position to make their own schedules or to turn down work. Everyone, however, can set priorities and make an effort to keep them as much as possible.

Look at your schedule and determine if you are being run by activities or by relationships.

THE "TOP FIVE"

Below is my "top five" list of treasures:

1. God
2. Kari
3. Michael and Hannah
4. Family
5. Helping others gain financial freedom
    so they can have a stronger relationship
    with Christ, spouse, and family.

I schedule my activities for the day according to how they affect these important relationships and the goals I have set for my life. That does not mean I spend every waking moment catering to the needs of my wife and kids. It does mean that — when a choice has to be made, between an activity and a relationship — Kari and my family come first.

Sure, earning income to support my family shows them I am caring for their material needs. In addition, whenever I go to the bank, stop for groceries on the way home, mow the lawn, etc. — all these mundane daily duties go toward strengthening our family and keeping our household running smoothly.

If, on the other hand, I decide to stop at a bookstore on the way home and spend hours browsing through investment books, I would have my priorities out of order. The banking would go undone, my family would have nothing to eat for dinner, and the grass would be too high for the kids to play outside.

One afternoon, I was working in my home office to complete this chapter for my book. According to my writing schedule, I had to finish it that day. When I heard Kari come home with Michael and Hannah, my concentration was broken by noisy chatter and giggling as the kids chased one another around the house. Apparently, they were still in a "fun" mode.

IN SEARCH OF OUR GREATEST COMMODITY

Kari stood in the office doorway with a look of "don't even ask me about my day!"

Obviously exasperated, she was silently pleading, "How about a little help?"

I tried to keep working, but I could hear the kids upstairs running around like wild monkeys. I had to make a decision. Do I drop number two on my priority list (Kari)? Or tend to number five (my work)?

Number two outweighs number five, so I shut down the computer and took the kids outside to play. (Good thing I was working on this chapter about priorities!)

In the past, I would have told Kari, "I'm working on a deadline, and I must finish writing this chapter today!" Then I would have yelled from my desk, "You kids settle down and be quiet!" Riddled with guilt, I would have continued to work, leaving my already exhausted wife to deal with the kids.

By choosing to put my marriage relationship first, I eliminated Kari's frustration and avoided potential conflict between us. To be relationship-driven provides continuous positive results; to be activity driven creates an endless negative impact.

FALLING INTO PLACE

"That idea sounds great," you may be saying, "and family should come first. But I can't ignore certain duties and activities."

During his seminars, Dr. Stephen Covey provides a great object lesson on how activities and relationships can mesh together. After selecting a volunteer from the audience, Dr. Covey brings him on stage and points to a big jar three-quarters full of marbles. "These represent activities," Dr. Covey explains.

Next to the jar on the table are several rocks of different sizes. "These

WE NEVER KNOW THE LOVE OF THE PARENT UNTIL WE BECOME PARENTS OURSELVES.

HENRY WARD BEECHER
(1813–1887)

represent priorities," he tells the volunteer.

"I want you to fit all the rocks into the jar without taking out any marbles," Dr. Covey instructs.

After several attempts the volunteer becomes very frustrated and is forced to leave out some of the rocks. "This is impossible," he complains as the audience laughs.

"I see," says Dr. Covey, "not all of your priorities will fit, will they?"

"No," the man replies.

Dr. Covey then empties the jar of the marbles onto the table.

"Try again to fit all the rocks into the jar," he tells the volunteer.

Without any difficulty, the man puts all the rocks in the jar.

Dr. Covey asks, "Can you fit anything else into the jar?"

The volunteer dumps the marbles into the jar. They all fit without overflowing!

What lesson can we learn from this demonstration? That once we prioritize what is important to us and schedule our priorities first, then the activities will fall into place and duties will be met.

GOD — THE BEST PLANNER

By planning, we are being Christ-like. Why? Because God is a planner. In fact, God planned you as well as all your days.

After Joseph interpreted Pharaoh's dream, he outlined a survival strategy to help Egypt avoid starvation (see Gen. 41:28-36). Joseph provided Pharaoh with a 14-year plan that began with Egypt receiving "a period of great prosperity throughout all the land of Egypt" for the first seven years. This would be followed by seven years of a famine so terrible "that the memory of the good years will be erased."

After explaining his dream and what was going to happen to the Egyptians, Joseph follows it up with this suggestion: "Find the wisest man in Egypt and put him in charge of administering a nationwide farm program. Let the Pharaoh divide Egypt into five administrative districts, and let the officials of the districts gather into the royal storehouse all the excess crops of the next seven years, so that there will be enough to eat when the seven years of famine come. Otherwise, disaster will surely strike."

Pharaoh liked the plan so much that he put Joseph in command of the nationwide farm program. Why? "For he is a man who is obviously filled with the Spirit of God." Joseph became a ruler because he was a planner.

Although Joseph experienced many heartaches in his life, his response to God was always the same: "What should I do now?" Instead of asking "Why?" he looked forward to the plan God had for him.

All true success in life results from first consulting God, and, second, by planning.

You may be asking, "What does this have to do with finances?" By planning first, we eliminate worry and frustration.

Didn't Christ say, "Don't be anxious for tomorrow?" Yes, but he wasn't talking about planning, he was talking about worry. Planning is thinking ahead about the goals, steps, and schedules that move you toward God's plan for your life.

Not having a plan says, "God, I don't know if I can trust You because I may not like what You have for me." Without a plan, life will be consumed with fear because it is difficult to trust God.

When planning is done right, however, it eliminates worry. Why? Because a plan is a written statement that says, "God, I trust in You, and I want You to direct my steps each day of my life."

INVESTING WHERE IT COUNTS

Well thought-out plans for the future eliminate financial pressure on your marriage and family. "Help me to prefer obedience to making money! Turn me away from wanting any other plan than yours" (Ps. 119:36-37). A plan keeps our eyes focused on Christ.

Frank and Judy did not have a plan to achieve their goals. As a result, Frank became a slave to the "things" they had dreamed of doing and owning before they were married.

A plan designed by both Frank and Judy would help them prioritize and schedule their days according to what is important to them. The plan would put this couple in alignment with each other because Frank would be pursuing the goals God had directed them to achieve.

The family mission statement (as outlined in chapter 6) is the agreement a husband and wife reach together through the direction of the Holy Spirit. It will be your map for financial decisions that impact the family.

And what is a family? A husband, wife, and children committed to building lifelong relationships together. After all, relationships are the essence of life.

What will happen to your marriage when the nest is empty and all your kids are out on their own? Do you and your mate have enough common ground to go it as a twosome? What if you lost all your money for some reason? How would that affect your marriage?

Now is the time to start investing in your marriage and family. If you do, the return will be well worth your time and effort.

In the next chapter, I want to tell you about another relationship with a great payoff — one that earns eternal dividends.

CHAPTER THIRTEEN
THE GREATEST INVESTMENT

BACK IN the early 1900s, a young boy set four goals he wanted to accomplish before he died:

1. Become the best movie producer.
2. Become a world-famous golfer.
3. Become one of the best aviators.
4. Become the richest man in the world.

Although these were lofty goals, the young man was determined to reach all four.

At the age of 19, his father passed away and left him in charge of the Hughes Tool Company, which owned the patent to an oil-drilling bit. During the oil boom, the company made lots of money.

At the age of 23, he became a Hollywood movie producer, winning a 1928 Academy Award for the film, *Two Arabian Knights*. He went on to produce many classics, including *Scarface* and *Hell's Angels* with Jean Harlow, *The Outlaw* with Jane Russell, *Stomboli* with Ingrid Bergman, and *The Conqueror* with John Wayne.

In his late twenties, Howard Hughes began his next challenge by starting his own aviation company, Hughes Aircraft, in Burbank, California. After hiring a small crew of engineers, designers, and mechanics, he concentrated on modifying military aircraft for racing.

By 1935, Howard Hughes set a new world speed record of 352 mph in an airplane. Three years later Hughes and four crew members accomplished another world record — an around-the-world flight in three days, 19 hours, and 14 minutes. The record received lots of publicity and made Howard Hughes one of the most famous men in America.

The record received special attention because just one year earlier Amelia Earhart had disappeared, and two years earlier Wiley Post and Will Rogers were killed attempting the same feat. For his accomplishment, Howard Hughes was given a New York City ticker-tape parade.

By the time Howard Hughes reached his late forties, he had become one of the richest men in the world. *Forbes Magazine* listed him second to J. Paul Getty as the richest person in the world. Hughes, who despised paying taxes, hid a lot of his holdings and was probably worth closer to $6 billion — three times as much as J. Paul Getty.

WEALTH IS

LIKE

SEAWATER;

THE MORE

WE DRINK,

THE

THIRSTIER

WE

BECOME;

THE SAME

IS TRUE OF

FAME.

ARTHUR
SCHOPENHAUER
(1788–1860)

Howard Hughes accomplished three of his four lofty, boyhood goals. (He fell far short of becoming a world-famous golfer.) The success of his accomplishments, however, were only temporary. In his last years, he became a lonely, paranoid recluse and drug addict with no friends or close family. He died in 1976.

Thousands of years earlier, a young prince was made king of his ancient nation and became the richest and most powerful man in the world. He wrote a journal that is included in the Bible — the Book of Ecclesiastes.

Solomon — like Hughes — took over from his father and also received early success. With all his wisdom, Solomon loved life. "And all that my eyes desired I did not refuse them. I did not withhold my heart from any pleasure" (Eccles. 2:10;NAS), he wrote. Solomon had over 300 wives, and his palace took 13 years to complete. He rebuilt the temple of Jerusalem, complete with gold-plated walls! What do these two gentlemen have in common? Wealth, intelligence, ambitious goals — and misery.

Late in life, King Solomon realized that money, possessions, and women were all "vanity" compared to pursuing a personal relationship with God. Contentment in life cannot be found unless God is at the center of your life. "The final conclusion, when all has been heard, is: fear God and keep his commandments, because this applies to every person" (Eccles. 12:13).

Like Howard Hughes and Solomon, most people would like to achieve success, wealth, and possessions. God, however, knows that the material things of this world will not satisfy the longings of our soul. Sure, we have physical desires and need money to buy things. Problems arise when we make striving to attain material possessions our main goal in life.

"Stop loving this evil world and all that it offers you, for when you love these things you show that you do not really love God; for all these worldly things, these evil desires — the craze for sex, the ambition to buy everything that appeals to you, and the pride that comes from wealth and importance — these are not from God. They are from this evil world itself" (1 John 2:15-16).

The apostle John warns us not to be consumed with "getting it all" in this temporary, earthly life. Why not? Because we will miss out on the really good stuff.

"Some of these people have missed the most important thing in life — they don't know God" (1 Tim. 6:21). When you don't know God — and it comes time for the final exam — I guarantee you will fail.

FOUR WORLDLY PURSUITS

A car commercial featuring the ultimate driving machine (possessions) focused on a beautiful, successful couple (people) parked outside a posh restaurant (prestige), where other happy, smiling adults were admiring their car (pleasure).

What message does this commercial convey? If you buy this car, you will have the ultimate possession, be surrounded by good-looking people, be classified with the prestigious, and be able to experience real pleasure.

Product marketers know it takes more than good merchandise to hook a buyer. They must convince their audience that their product offers the intangibles of power, prestige, and pleasure. The sense of fulfillment sells the product.

The most effective commercials combine all four of these worldly pursuits: pleasure, prestige, possession, and people.

Let's look at these four categories:

1. Pleasure.

Whenever a comedian dies — no matter how lousy a guy he was — the media always quips, "He made people laugh." That seems to be everyone's chief goal in life.

The entertainment industry has become a multi-billion dollar business. Americans are consumed with the idea that watching television, going to the movies, or seeing a Broadway play provides a sense of fulfillment.

Disney makes billions of dollars making people happy — or at least that's what they want us to believe. If your kid doesn't have the latest Disney video, his childhood will be ruined.

We often turn to the world in an effort to find happiness and often seek it by looking into the pleasure category. However, like Moses, we make a better choice when we opt to stand "with God's people instead of enjoying the fleeting pleasures of sin" (Heb. 11:25).

2. Prestige.

We are a status-driven society. Designer clothes, foreign cars, and job titles allow us to determine where people fall — like hens — in the pecking order. We buy clothes with labels on the outside to advertise the fact we are wearing something expensive. "He must be well-off financially, if he can afford to pay that much for a shirt!" we imagine them saying.

Some people work their lives away to achieve a job title that offers prestige in the community. Wives can sometimes pressure husbands to improve their job status. At the same time, husbands may force their wives into becoming the perfect company hostess.

Prestige is another form of power. Many people think that the higher the position in life, the more fulfilling life will be.

3. Possessions.

Many people are tormented by the thought: *If only I had one of those!*

If I had a boat, I could go fishing every weekend. Then I would be really happy.

If I had a new BMW, I would never have to worry anymore about car repairs.

The Greatest Investment

If I had a nicer house, I could have all the latest conveniences.

All these things bring a certain amount of satisfaction. That joy soon dissipates, however, when we see the bigger boat, the fancier car, and the more elegant house that our neighbor owns. Then our desires rise to the next higher level, and we are no longer content.

When one mate is driven to find happiness in possessions, it can put terrible strain on the marriage — both emotionally, spiritually, and financially.

4. People.

Seeking the acceptance of people to give us meaning and fulfillment only leads to troubled relationships. The facts are: No one is perfect, and not everyone is going to love and accept you.

Those who look to people for their happiness, live frustrated lives.

"When I find the right husband, I will be happy."

"If I got divorced, I would be happy."

"If I wear this outfit, the girls at work will admire me."

"If I can lose ten pounds, maybe my husband will appreciate me."

"If I get another degree, my boss will promote me."

When we feel depressed, we often look to people to give us a shot of encouragement. When something goes well for us, we want people to congratulate us. When they don't, we blame them for ruining our moment.

So what happens when you are sick of going to movies, tired of trying to impress everyone, own more things

MY RICHES

CONSIST

NOT IN THE

EXTENT OF

MY

POSSESSIONS

BUT IN THE

FEWNESS OF

MY WANTS.

JOSEPH
BROTHERTON
(1783–1857)

than you can pay for, and have alienated your family and friends?

Is that all there is? If we can't get our fill from pleasure, prestige, possessions, and people — how will we ever find contentment?

THE SECRET TO FULFILLMENT

Jesus, who lived and walked among mankind for 33 years, observed firsthand the emptiness that people experience in this life.

That's why He provided us with the answer: "But seek first his kingdom and his righteousness, and all these things will be given to you as well" (Matt. 6:33;NIV).

My entire life revolves around this verse. If I go to God and seek His ways, then everything else will be given to me. The Father promises to be the provider of everything we need. I am not talking about material things; I am talking about a life full of purpose and satisfaction. God is asking us to get to know Him, to seek Him and His righteousness, and then everything we need will be added to us.

The first ingredient to a life that is full of love, joy, and peace is to have Jesus Christ in your life. This is how the apostle John puts it: "And what is it that God has said? That he has given us eternal *life*, and that this *life* is in his Son. So whoever has God's Son has *life*; whoever does not have his Son, does not have *life*" (1 John 5:11-12, italics added).

The word "life" is mentioned four times in these two verses.

1. Life is about having eternal *life.*
2. You can have eternal *life* by accepting
   Jesus Christ into your life.
3. By having Christ in your life, you gain
   life.
4. Without Christ in your life, you have no
   life.

I guess that says it all. Now it's up to you to receive the eternal life that God has promised through His Son Jesus Christ. Then this life will become more exciting and enjoyable than you could ever dream.

NEVER ENOUGH

If you feel that you have let money, possessions, or your mate get in the way of your happiness, turn to God and ask Him to become the center of your life. The Scripture says, "The worries of this life, the deceitfulness of wealth and the desires for other things come in and choke the word" (Mark 4:19;NIV).

If you are a slave to the Four P's — possessions, prestige, pleasure, and people — they will never be enough. Once you have achieved your worldly goals, someone or something will always come along and top what you have done.

Whenever we allow our focus to get off of the prize — Jesus Christ — our need for fulfillment has to come from somewhere or someone else. When that happens, you are guaranteed only one thing: misery.

Ultimate fulfillment comes from our heavenly Father: "May your roots go down deep into the soil of God's marvelous love; and may you be able to feel and understand, as all God's children should, how long, how wide, how deep, and how high his love really is; and to experience this love for yourselves, though it is so great that you will never see the end of it or fully know or understand it. And so at last you will be filled up with God himself" (Eph. 3:17-19).

God has created mankind with a thirst that only He can fill. No matter how rich or beautiful or famous you are, you will never find true joy in people, possessions, prestige, or pleasure.

Howard Hughes may have been a great aviator, but somewhere along the way, his life went off-course. The next time you and your mate hit financial turbulence, check your instrument panel to see where you are headed — toward one of the four P's — or toward the Cross.

ENDNOTES

Chapter Two
[1]Gary Smalley and John Trent, *Two Sides of Love* (Colorado Springs, CO: Focus on the Family, 1990).

[2]Tim LaHaye, Jerry and Ramona Tuma, *Smart Money* (Sisters, OR: Multnomah Books, 1994).

Chapter Three
[1]Forbes, April 21, 1997.

Chapter Four
[1]Faith Popcorn and Lys Marigold, *Clicking* (New York, NY: Harper Collins, 1996).

Chapter Five
[1]Howard Markman, Scott Stanley, and Susan L. Blumberg, *Fighting for Your Marriage* (San Francisco, CA: Jossey-Bass Publishing, 1994).

[2]Gary Smalley and John Trent, *The Language of Love* (Colorado Springs, CO: Focus on the Family, 1988).

Chapter Six
[1]R. Kent Hughes, *1001 Great Stories and Quotes* (Wheaton, IL: Tyndale House Publishers, 1998).

[2]Gary Smalley and John Trent, *The Hidden Value of a Man* (Colorado Springs, CO: Focus on the Family, 1992).

[3]James C. Collins and Jerry I. Porras, *Built to Last* (New York City, NY: Harper Business, 1994).

Chapter Seven
[1]Ron Blue, *Mastering Your Money* (Nashville, TN: Thomas Nelson Publishers, 1991).

[2]Ron Blue, *Storm Shelter* (Nashville, TN: Thomas Nelson Publishers, 1994).

Chapter Eight
[1]Kathy Keistof, *Money,* February 1998, p. 147.

[2]Adriane Berg, *Financial Planning for Couples* (New York City, NY: Newmarket Press, 1988), p. 132.

You can bring an exciting seminar on

First Comes Love, Then Comes Money

to your church or community! Roger Gibson will share insights on keys to resolving the #1 conflict in marriage: finances. Roger will show you how to get rid of the marriage monster, help you discover your money personality, and learn the secret to an investment that pays a lifetime of dividends and more.

For more information, or to schedule a seminar, contact:

Eagle Family Ministries
210 N. Walton Blvd., Suite 30
P.O. Box 488
Bentonville, AR 72712
Phone: (501) 464-4442
Fax: (501) 464-9210
E-mail: eaglefamilyministries@juno.com